Intermediate Guide to Japanese Joinery

Jin Izuhara

Table of Contents

Introduction

Reading this and implementing its techniques will make you a pro in Japanese joinery. This guide is based on the renowned aspects of traditional Japanese joinery. s. The tools used in Japanese joinery are most important to the beauty of the carpentry. The product of seemingly mystical differences, such as the tool used on the pull-stroke, cannot be undervalued. The wide use of hand planes, and the tempering achievable by their wood frames, is a crucial aspect of how these specific tools stimulate a stealthy craft culture.

This particular aspect gave rise to the closer relationship between material and maker. The extensive use of fire and water as instruments shines effervescent light on the deep knowledge Japanese joinery artists have for their medium. How wood expands when moist is a property embraced by the carpenter.

The topics explored in this book include: Japanese joinery, tools and tool maintenance workspaces, advanced joints, and intermediate skill level shading techniques. When finished, you will have crafted five extremely beautiful projects with precise accuracy as absolutely remarkable decor to compliment your house, office, or any space you desire to embellish. The projects set forth in this book follow progressively, so your skills can continue to advance as they build upon the next. By the end of this book, you will be well-equipped with the fundamentals of Japanese joinery, a further understanding of timber, advanced joint making techniques, and an understanding of the self-discipline that is so essential in the craft. The foundation provided in these teachings is there, so you can take the knowledge and further yourself.

The projects in this book offer details of Japanese joinery and how to craft it. It is a hands-on, step-by-step directive of how these structures are done in actuality by Japanese carpenters. Sharpen your tools and get ready to work with these techniques for your own personal projects.

The philosophies behind the process that Japanese woodworkers adhere to have profound results on the products they create. The most notable of these philosophical schools of thought is having a quiet or silent environment and lightness of touch while crafting. The noise is kept down by keeping pieces apart from one another, and the material is light in weight, a selection mastered by being attentive in choosing lumber, including bamboo.

The philosophies, strategies, and tools of Japanese joinery, and the respect for the skill, have created a lasting and contemporary style. One difference between Japanese joinery and Western carpentry is the philosophy regarding showing joints. Many Western woodcrafters choose to "exhibit" their skill by showing their joint work. The Japanese woodcrafting philosophy is to hide the joints by using wedged tenons and dovetails. Here, the only joints exposed emphasize a joint's labor in holding weight; for instance, in a chair's design. In this case, the joints would be visible where the seat rails are attached to the front and rear legs. The other reason for hiding the joints is so the beauty of the timber remains the most important. Another interesting reason for hiding joints is if they might protrude slightly due to dampness. The would hide the joints at a 90-degree angle, so the line of intersection bisects the angle. The joints therefore, become less susceptible to moisture and can work smoothly all year around.

Circle the answer to the following multiple choice question: Which is a characteristic of Japanese joinery?

1. Exposing the joints by using wedged tenons and dovetails.
2. Hiding the joints at a 60-degree angle, so that the line of intersection bisects the angle and the joints become less susceptible to moisture.
3. One of the hardest challenges in pursuing Japanese joinery can be having the will to embrace all of the teachings.
4. There is very little need for practicing Japanese joinery, since people usually get it right the first time.
5. None of the above.
6. All of the above.

Chapter One: Japanese Joinery, Tools and Workspace

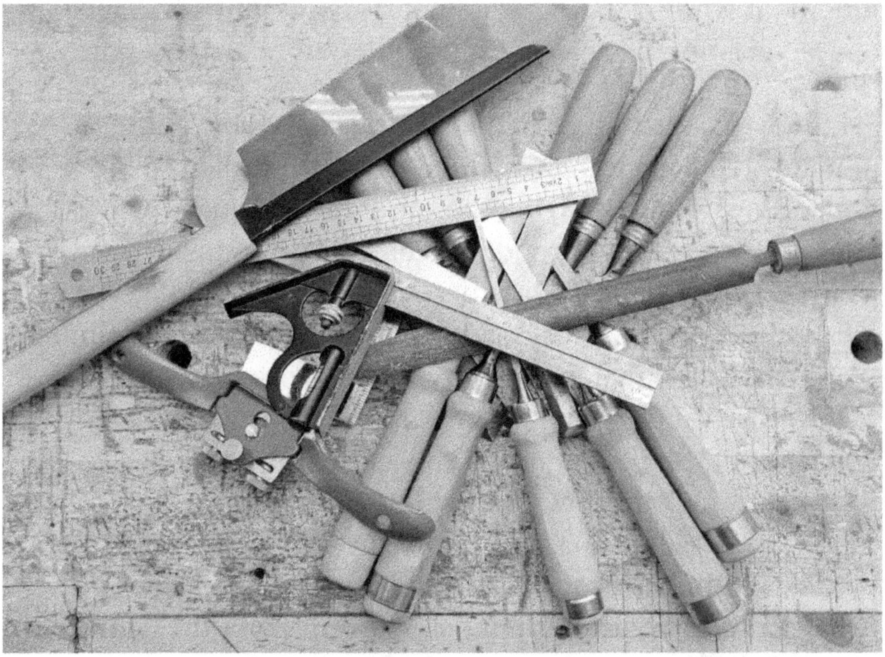

If you looked up Japanese joinery now, you will find a multitude of videos and essays discussing complex work pieces and joints. But this book is not geared for reading about someone else's work; this intermediate guide will aid you in enjoying touching the wood, smoothing the surface with a hand plane, and putting pieces that you have crafted together with your own two hands. Through step-by-step tutorial projects, you will advance your knowledge and skill of Japanese joinery and learn to craft more complex designs than before as a beginner. Don't panic if you think they look complicated—the steps we will go over will be easy to understand. No matter how complicated it may look, the result of every step, when done as instructed, will make it possible to achieve any challenging goal successfully. You don't necessarily have to be super coordinated, but you do need perseverance. Certain wood crafting techniques try to fix disadvantages forcefully by grinding the timber and glueing it while destroying its natural and unique characteristics, basically resulting in chipboard.

Such disadvantages include burles—or *moku* in Japanese—by grinding the wood finely, and then fixing it with adhesives, destroying the inherent, unique characteristics of the wood. The end result of this is known as MDF, or chipboard. Japanese joinery is about getting to know and working with the different personalities of timber. At its essence, Japanese joinery recognizes every piece of timber as a unique, living element and finds a creative way to bring about the best in each. This is the foundation of the woodworking tradition. For example, homestyle meals that grandmothers have passed down through generations are, of course, better than processed and prefabricated meals. Likewise, chipboard has almost no scent from the beautiful piece of timber it once was. It has lost its inherent personality by bending to human will.

One may ask why Japanese joinery uses less adhesives and fewer nails. It is because metal rusts, first of all, and timber starts to rot when the screws or nails rust. Nails are also not sufficient in harboring the movement of the wood. Wood moves constantly with changes in the environment and the seasons. Japanese joinery is closely analyzing the differences in each piece of timber and connecting them, so when they try to move in different directions, they keep each other still and stable.

The problems with using so much glue is that it removes the ability of the timber to breathe. These days, we have developed adhesives so strong that they can pick up a car. That is exactly the problem, since wood is always moving and wants to keep moving. For instance, you glued two pieces of timber together vertically, then glued the edges in place with a strong glue (i.e. super, gorilla, etc.). You may think you did a great job until the middle sections of the planks started wanting to move. They want to expand when it is humid and contract when it's cold. If these changes occur, and the edges of the planks are restricted in movement... *CRACK!* They will probably split right down the center. Moving parts are important for wood, just like they are for people. Most of all, it is very enjoyable to construct a piece through your own ingenuity. Creating a framework formation using a saw, plane, chisel, your imagination, and your own two hands into something that is joined together with other pieces to form one solid structure is a rather satisfying accomplishment.

Modern day engineering of timber is an example of society's will to eradicate anything inconsistent or unpredictable. In Japanese joinery, wood crafting is tightly managed. Most historical buildings in Japan exhibit standards in their construction by repeating glue the elements, and there, century-old structures still remain in good condition. Craftsmen practicing joinery techniques exert mastery over the timber and other such materials' behaviors. However, the way they do it is considerably different from Western industrial methods. Rather than eliminating materials that vary in strength according to the direction of their measurements (i.e. plywood), Japanese joinery crafters go to great lengths to take advantage of these specific traits. Not only does the practice with timber's innate grain by methodically positioning structural pieces make strong connections and prevent sag, but it also utilizes the timber's original state to its advantage, such as using a north-facing tree on the north side of a house (Brownell, 2016). Furthermore, crafters design specifics that project the timber's inescapable transformation over millennia, compensating for deviation and constriction.

Such skill shows profound mastery over timber and extraordinary technological finesse. A common thought is that old structures are physically inferior to modern steel and concrete fabrications, yet this is debatable. First of all, the quality of the materials used are often inferior. A manufactured wood beam pales in comparison to a single log of hickory or cypress. Historical methods for processing timber are more rigorous than modern manufacturing methods. What should be challenged today is the possibility that expediency in contemporary construction contributes to material decline. With the recent rallying of interest in structures made of wood, Japanese joinery offers inspiration for future, wood-based construction methods. Western carpentry would benefit from a better appreciation of timber origins, its deployment, and behavior over long periods of time (Brownell, 2016). Various factors give rise to irregular and complicated patterns in timber.

Moku (Burls)

There is *tama-moku* (circular burl), *budo-moku* (grape burl), *sasa-moku* (bamboo leaf burl), and *uzura-moku* (quail feather burl).

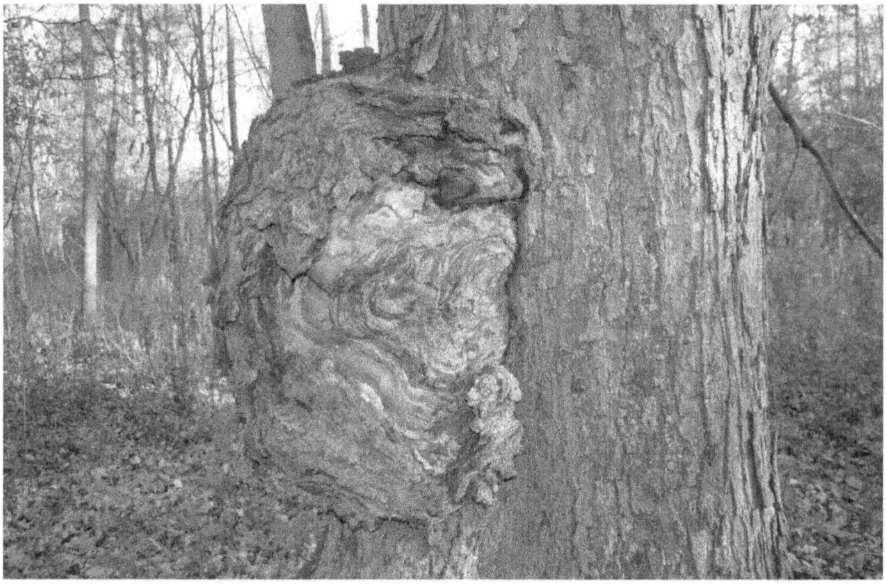

Moku (burls) are bulb-like growths on timber, usually as a result of an injury to the tree (see the image above). These *moku* make for eye-catching accents, specifically as handles, veneers, inlays, and more. For this reason, *moku* are extremely valuable in the world of Japanese joinery. If you are fortunate enough to stumble across a tree that is down and has burls, you can cut large sections of it, including at least six inches of the trunk material either above or below the *moku*. Being encased by the extra timber protects the *moku* from drying out too quickly. Try to save as much of the *moku's* figure as possible. Do not slice it from the trunk—unless it is too big to handle—but slice through the meat and take off the back half of the trunk, which will make it lighter and smaller. For transporting noticeably large *moku*, cut them into manageable pieces while still allowing extra material.

If you are cutting *moku* into planks, cut 25% thicker than necessary, so there is room for change during drying. Also, depending on the grain of the *moku*, the direction you cut can make a change in the appearance. *Moku* usually have a random swirling or eye figure grain. To dry them faster, trim and size the *moku*. If you are not in a rush to use it, you can also slowly let them air dry. With this method, they can produce changes in their color and spalting (change in wood color caused by fungi), adding extra character to the piece. The only way to tell if the *moku* has an eye figure is to trim a thin slick from the top of the *moku*. Eye figures in the *moku* are generally found in walnut, maple, ash, and cherry trees. Swirling grains in moku are usually found in birch, gum, and mulberry. Using end grain sealer for wood, cover the exposed ends. Make sure to store it away from direct sunlight and rain. Thick pieces of *moku* can take up to six months to dry, whereas, ¾-inch planks take four months when stored in a warm environment (Hoover, 2020).

Steps for Cutting Rounds in Moku

1. Using a chainsaw, cut through the pith of the oversized section and remove the back half of the piece, while also making the back of the *moku* flat.

2. Trim any excess trunk ends. Chainsaw the sides of the *moku* to make it square.

3. Make a disc out of cardboard as a guide for cutting the *moku's* top.

4. Using your band saw and cardboard disc, complete the round.

Timber

Wood needs to dry for several years after being cut down. It is then processed (*kidori*) according to its need. In Japanese joinery, timber can be cut across (*itame-dori*) or with the grain (*masame-dori*). The growth rings in with the grain (*masame-dori*) cuts appear on the surface as a series of parallel lines. When cut across the grain (*itame-dori*), it appears as irregular patterns. When the timber is removed from the outer part of the tree, the grain is glossier and more attractive than if it was taken closer to the center.

Japanese Joinery Tools

Joinery tools are used mainly on a pull-stroke control, rather than the Western push-stroke technique. With a wooden bodied hammer (*Kanna*), adjusted planes are pulled toward the worker in order to make the cut. Likewise, Japanese saws' (*nokogiri*) teeth are angled toward the worker, so they meet with the timber fibers with the pull stroke. When it comes to saws, the pull stroke has an extensive effect on the tool's build. Western saws have to resist the buckling intensity of cutting on the push stroke. The motion of pulling a Japanese saw through the cut results in the blade tensioning naturally. This saw also has better accuracy because of its thin blade. The fine blade promotes precise and delicate cuts. The quickness matched with the precision of the cut advances a wider use of hand-saws used in joinery.

Circle the right answer: Which of the following saws makes cross cuts and bevels?

A. Radial.

B. Compound miter.

C. Hack.

D. Air.

Japanese hammer ("Genno" or "Gennoh" 玄能): There are various types of Japanese hammers; some are used to position hand plane blades, some are used for chiseling, some for pounding out steel that had been hardened by lacquer, and some just for hammering nails.

Dead-blow mallet: A hammer hollowed out and filled with steel. It aids the crafter in delivering controlled and solid blows to the piece. The large head widens the force over a wide area, making it perfect for joints.

Japanese gimlet (kiri 錐): The kiri is used for hollowing out circular holes in a piece of wood, which is usually the first step in boring out a mortise. Although it may seem simple to use, the Japanese gimlet is considered a very difficult tool to master.

Japanese saws (nokogiri 鋸): The *nokogiri* uses a pull stroke to cut, allowing the blades to be much thinner than what Western saws have. The two principal types of cutting teeth are the rip (*tatebiki*) and the crosscut (*yokobiki*). There are various other types of Japanese saws used in joinery too, such as the stiff-backed saw (*jdouzuki*), ridge saw (*azebiki*), press-cut saw, (*osae-biki*) among others.

Inkpot (sumitsubo 墨壺): The inkpot is used for marking lengthy straight lines onto varying wood surfaces. A piece of thread is fastened to a round wood piece, with a needle attached at the end. The opposite end of the thread is inserted through the small opening at the end of the inkpot through a pit containing ink. It is then wrapped around a spool. The ink is kept in an ink-soaked silk wadding (Butler, 2004). The silk threads are used to draw lines by holding the inkpot (*sumitsubo*) in one's left hand, positioning the thread onto the surface, and slowly moving away until the measured degree of thread is unraveled, at which point you would press your thumb down to stop the reeling. Then, with one's index finger, they would press the thread down to the measured end point of the line. Using one's right hand, they would pull the thread upward until it is tense, then suddenly release, leaving the line straight on any surface, even if it has irregularities.

Blades

In Japanese joinery, blades are made by steel smiths and are unmounted, so the carpenter can fashion the handles by their own hands. In Japan, steel has always been crafted with a high level of refinement, for without, the detail and beautiful surface work in Japanese joinery could not be accomplished. Similar to the Japanese chisel and plane, the edge of these blades are extremely thin, hard, and welded to a softer metal piece to function as a shock absorber and protect the tip from breakage. This traditional albeit advanced technology permits the use of harder steel and sharpening of a much finer edge. In Japanese joinery, it is customary to go through at least three whetstones that vary in coarseness, moving from the roughest to the finest stone. The blade of both chisels and planes are noted by the hollow sole on their flat sides. This portion makes sure there is a high degree of flatness when sharpened. Note that when the flat side is burnished, it cannot develop curves or rock, as it is the only contact with the whetstone. This advances the precision of the cuts made by the chisel and ensures a smoother contact with the wedge. It thus produces an even degree of support to scroll the entire width of the blade. The hollow sole also vastly lowers the amount of steel needed to be taken out to acquire flatness on the back side of the blade, lessening the need for resharpening.

When it comes to chisels, the blades reduce the resistance to friction as it is pounded into or taken out of the timber. Also, the interaction between the blade and leading edge is a relationship that changes as the blade is resharpened. With the blades on planes, as the edge is honed down to the hollow's rim, it can then be pushed out—a process called *ura-dashi*, where a pointed hammer pushes in the blade slightly downward along the bevel. The back of the blade is flattened again, after which the hollow is reestablished. This process acts as a gauging mechanism for sharpening and prolonging the life of a thin blade. It also keeps consistent measurements of the blade over time. There are various steel types used for Japanese chisels and planes. White steel (*shiro-gane*) is almost pure steel that resharpens easily. Blue steel (*ao-gane*) is a bit harder to sharpen than white steel, but it is sturdier.

Planes

It is the act of pulling the plane into the body that makes this tool successful. In traditional Japanese joinery, woodworkers would work on the floor, which allowed the worker to generate more power from their sitting position. Sitting also increased the worker's control and enactment with the timber and fosters a more controlled, careful engagement with it. The act of pushing a tool through a material requires an explosive thrust of force. The further away they are from the worker's body, the less control. It is also more difficult to see the shaving made, which is a valuable measure of the cut-quality achieved. Japanese planes are drawn toward the body; therefore, they can control their cutting better, and the shavings are always visible. The plane's wooden body gives the joiner unspoken knowledge. For instance, the density and difficult grains can be felt more through the body.

Knives

Surprisingly, the knivery used in Japanese joinery also employs a pull-stroke. In basket-making, the known technique in preparing the bamboo is for the knife to be gripped against the crafter's knee, and then the bamboo would be pulled along the blade. The bamboo is supported by a block of wood, which helps ensure the thickness of the cut. Pulling the knife makes a thinner and finer medium to be worked with. It also keeps the eye of the user on the exposed blade. Lastly, the maker has a better feel of the stress the knife is subject to and can change their technique accordingly. The pull-stroke is one of the main differences between Japanese and Western woodworking. It is comprehensive in its effect—that is, in the tools' anatomy, how they are experienced, the size and species of the wood, and in what clues are fed to the user during the project. Research on the Japanese pull-stroke found that users felt more control, had better accuracy, required less effort, and were given more subtle information (Ryokogyo, 2020; Sennet, 2008; Toshio, 2006).

Vises

Vises used in Japanese joinery are wedges of timber tied to a pylon with a loop of rope. The timber is then put under the wedge, and the wedge is pounded down with a hammer. Vises are used much less in Japanese joinery than in Western carpentry.

Techniques with Water

Water is actually a tool used frequently in Japanese joinery, unlike in the West, where it is feared. Wood is composed of a bundle of tube-like patterns running up and down the tree. These tubes have a lot of water in them, which adds to its weight. In order to use the tree's gift of wood, the water needs to be removed through aeration or dried in a kiln. This way, the timber is stable and strong. Interestingly, the tubes do not lose their ability to re-take up moisture. When left in a wet environment, dry wood will absorb water until it is equal to the moisture of the environment within which it dwells. That is why crafters usually try to keep their wood from being exposed to moisture. In Japanese joinery, water plays a more harmonized role, evident in the utilization of waterstones to sharpen items, where the moisture lubricates the sharp particles of finely grained sedimentary stone. Today, waterstones are used widely in Western shops and made synthetically in circular forms for use in electrical sharpening equipment. In Japanese joinery, water is used in a much more detailed process other than just sharpening.

Stream-bending

Stream-bending is a technique whereby a piece of wood—if you were making a bowl—would be oval shaped. It is then soaked for three days in water. Then, the wood is microwaved for three minutes, which allows steam to form. This process makes the wood flexible and easily bendable. The timber is then placed in a shallow curve holder to form the shape. When the wood dries, the shape is set, resulting in an elegant serving dish. It may sound easy, but not necessarily. The technique is based on a tried and true method forged in experience and shared throughout the trade (Sugawara, 2020). The soaking time, temperature of the water, time in the microwave, and thickness of the wood are all finely balanced.

A more common use of water is when planing. The crafter always wants to plane in the direction of the timber grain, which helps them avoid tear-out and the necessity of having to use a chip breaker or sharper blade, or needing to change the direction to lower the cut's angle. One method used in Japanese joinery is to mist the surface of the wood and let it sit for several minutes. This technique allows the wood fibers to plump, lending itself to an easier cut. One problem with this method for Western woodworkers is the steel's potential to rust, which is used in manufacturing Western planes. Japanese planes are made of wood, and therefore do not have this problem. Western woodworkers may choose to dust their planes with oiled leather.

Fire Techniques

Heat and fire are interesting techniques used in Japanese joinery. The surface of wood when burned has unique properties. When charred, timber has protection from moisture. Also, the char adds a deep, rich, and dark color. One use of charred wood in Japanese woodcraftery is making use of "charred bamboo." Traditionally, the wood was acquired from the fireplace ceiling in Japanese kitchens. The smoke created by the fire would harden and dry the bamboo roof structures, making it a prized material often seen in crafted chopsticks. The reason smoked bamboo is good for chopsticks is that the wood has become stiff; however, that also makes it a bit difficult to work with.

Tool Modification

It is not an uncommon occurrence to see a one-of-a-kind tool in the kit of a Japanese woodworker. Tools are often personalized and modified to fit the work required and produced. Sometimes, it is just to make them a more comfortable fit. On some occasions, hammer heads are purchased by themselves because the crafter wants to make their own wooden handle. That way, the handle will fit the woodworker's grip perfectly. The woodcrafter may also want to change the distance between the handle and hammer head; therefore, changing the power can then be registered. Plane modifications are most apparent due to the timber bodies that hold the blade in place. Concave furrows allow the plane to move over roughly-sawn surfaces better, thus allowing it to be flattened faster.

Tools used to be very high priced back in the 50's, so woodcrafters had to learn how to do their own metal work. This legacy is still passed on to younger woodworkers through apprenticeships in the present day (Keller, 2020). One of the best features of Japanese joinery tools is that they are cordless!

Sandpaper

It is much more common in Japanese joinery to use blades and planes to smooth and level wood to its final finish. However, sandpaper made from a horsetail plant creates a very fine sandpaper that also polishes. The result of slicing the wood to result in the finished surface is better than a scratched up finish. Sandpaper is quicker, but physically passing a blade over the surface makes their silky smooth finish, which is easily recognizable when compared to sandpaper finishes.

Profiled planes add texture to a wood finish. Woodcrafters and others viewing planned finishes generally have an appreciation for the skill involved in creating it. In essence, it is the crafter's fingerprint. Japanese woodcrafters use sandpaper to remove sharp edges from their finished works.

Tool Maintenance

Ingrained in Japanese joinery is the concept of maintenance, which is, by itself, an art. Of great importance in Japanese woodcrafting is the workers' acceptance of continuous maintenance. This also ensures the passing on of crafting skills to future generations. Timber, due to its ability to become damaged by moisture, has a unique aspect when it comes to maintenance.

Lightness

Lightness in the craft is a theme present in Japanese joinery's philosophical background. Sometimes, this was considered in the species of wood, though other times it was the details employed in the construction or the careful design, which gained the desired effect. Lightness is important to the Japanese woodcrafter because it shows great respect for the value of timber while making it more affordable and efficient. Your craftsmanship should add to the harmony of your home rather than sticking out like a sore thumb. The crafter's search for lightness, in this concept, is the search for harmony that complements a space.

Circle true or false: You can only use hand tools for Japanese joinery.

Recommended Tools

With the right set of tools, you can realistically achieve the skills for the projects described in this book. Practicing joinery by hand will definitely advance your potential and give rise to more confidence with machinery. Although you may already have a nice set of tools the following are recommended:

a. Both a big and regular-sized hammer.

b. Carpenter's square and try square.

c. Bevel gauge.

d. Razor saw (ryoba nokogiri).

e. 24mm paring chisel (tsuki nomi).

f. 24mm striking chisel (tataki nomi).

g. 12mm striking chisel (tataki nomi).

h. 48mm hand plane (kanna).

i. 70mm hand plane (kanna).

j. 36mm shoulder plane (kiwa kanna).

k. Left and right metal plates.

l. Diamond plate.

m. Sharpening stone.

Chapter Two:
Advanced Joints

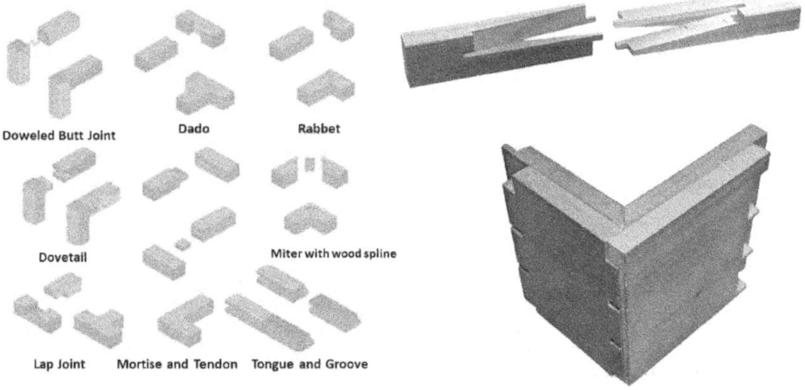

When contemplating wooden construction, it is usually along the lines of horizontal and post-architecture, with all the elements coming together at right angles. However, there are many structures in which the significance is placed on curved surfaces or diagonal elements.

In Japanese joinery, most of the construction uses straight lines. This is primarily due to the nature and characteristics of timber and its growth. The obvious deviations, of course, include curve-shaped kitchen utensils and smoothly curved furnishings, sometimes formed from a single timber piece. In these cases, Japanese joinery is the development of techniques to pressure wood into taking and retaining unnatural shapes. In addition to the vast variety of wood species available, you can pick the timber best suited for your intended use. In this craft, a joint is either a connecting joint (*shiguchi*) or splicing joint (*tsugite*), where in the West, joints are categorized in how the timber pieces are joined. In Japanese joinery, joints are categorized by the way they function. For example, two pieces of timber joined together end to end is referred to as a lap joint, or *tsugite*. A *tsugite* used to join two elements at a 90-degree angle is a connecting joint, or *shiguchi*. A *tsugite* and a *shiguchi* serve more of a purpose than holding wood together; they contribute both to the timber's elegance and its strength.

As you know from the Beginner's Guide to Japanese Joinery, it can be very difficult to get miters to close, or a three-way miter with interlocking tenons you can't even see to close. However, it is inspiring to see a 16-inch long miter connected together with dovetails disappeared, leaving no gaps on the outside or inside corners. Your road toward intermediate competency—leading to mastery—is long, though worth the work. As you move forward to an intermediate skill level, understanding joining systems is necessary to undertake the projects detailed in the following chapters.

Circle the hand tool used to shape timber using only your muscle strength.

A. Bench plane.

B. Bench saw.

C. Electric saw.

D. Saw plane.

Miter Joints

From an artistic viewpoint, the mither joint is an eye-pleasing concept for dealing with corners. It gives the onlooker the sense that there is continuous grain around the corners of an object. It is a sophisticated technique that needs a good deal of precision to be well-executed. Most frames, moldings, and other structures meet at a right angle of 90 degrees; therefore, 45 degrees would be the most common agle. In order for them to look good and be effective, they have to fit together perfectly. The most minor inaccuracy will not only affect the function but the strength and appearance of the miter joint.

Constructing a miter joint is something a woodcrafter of intermediate skill should no longer be struggling with. Any structure made using two or more pieces of lumber has a miter joint. It is constructed by joining two edges at a 45-degree angle on the face of the timber. This way, the timber's end grain stays hidden. Exactness is crucial, and a perfect miter calls for a careful setup with almost monotonous adjustments to follow. Most interestingly, with Japanese joinery techniques, a hand saw will be more accurate because cutting miters with machines causes forces on the material to push it away from the saw blade, which then causes the piece to move slightly. If this happens, it will affect the precision the crafter is working so hard to attain. When hand-marking your lumber for a 45-degree cut, use a miter box and tenon saw to cut the angle. Then, use a miter shooting board (at one edge is a shallow, wide rabbet where a plane rides; the rabbet bed supports the side wing, and the shoulder guides the plane) and a bench plane to rig the face of the miter, then adjust for inaccuracies. The many tools used for constructing miter joints will depend on your project. For a basic cut, a miter box and hand saw will be all you need. For more complicated miter cuts, various types of saws will come in handy, such as compound miter, radial-arm, table, or circular saws.

Tip: While a structure's mitered corners may look great, they can be difficult to clamp. A remedy for this situation is to add a spline across the joint. A spline will keep the joints aligned exactly during assembly.

Pinned Right Angle Miter Joint

Two conditions must be met for cutting clean and tight miters. At each end of the joint, the angle cut has to be the same and add up to the corner angle desired (a 90-degree angle needs two 45-degree miter cuts) and, for a rectangular or square project, the opposing pairs of parts' length must be exactly the same. You may find yourself with troubling, out-of-square corners (i.e. bumps on the surface). The trick to creating tight-fitting miters is understanding how to adjust your cuttery to real-world situations.

Miters usually need to be shaved in order to fit. One method is to adjust the angle just a bit on your miter saw, or simply place a thin piece of material against the saw fence to readjust the angle. Move the material closer to the blade for large adjustments and closer for smaller adjustments. Remember to cut the pieces exactly the same. Regardless of the technique or material used, accuracy is of utmost importance. Discrepancies—no matter how small—in the angle of mitered pieces can end up causing gaps in the joints, either at the base or in the tip. To avoid mistakes, cut a pair of samples. Put the sample pieces together with the biggest angle gauge you have and check your cuts. If they are off at all, there will be a visible gap in the corner.

Mitered pieces can be fastened together with glue, as both the plywood and solid pieces have partial saw blade tooth markings. Using glue actually produces enough strength to hold together items such as picture frames and small gifts. However, using glue can be tricky, since pieces can slip from their positions during the process. Using clamps to apply pressure to all sides is one remedy. When using pipe or bar clamps, it is helpful to drive a small nail into the joint at each corner to keep the parts in place.

Biscuit Joints

One of the lesser-known joinery joints is the biscuit joint, most likely because there are fewer places where you will find this joint to be more useful than other types. The joint got its name due to how the pieces of wood resemble the shape of a biscuit.

These particular joints strengthen and prevent the joint from moving. The biscuit joiner is a tool used to make the round (biscuit) shaped holes in the timber. The biscuit joint's main use is to connect wood boards together, such as table tops, and once secured, they are rather pleasing to the eye. They are quick to cut and easy to mark, but they may not be as sturdy as some of the other joints discussed in this book. Despite that, they are still suitable for many projects. They are strong, versatile, and used in various types of assemblies and for alignment problems. The best way to appreciate this versatile joint is by putting it to use. The size and shape of the biscuit joint makes it better than a dowel. It has an oversized slot, which allows the biscuit to move slightly, allowing you to adjust parts into their perfect alignments. However, once they are glued, the joint will swell, and the parts will be locked in place. The safest way to cut biscuit slots is with a biscuit joiner. This tool is designed to do nothing but plunge-cut arc-shaped slots. Unlike the router/biscuit-cutting bit combo, the biscuit joiner's cutter retracts inside the tool as you pull it away from your work.

From there, a flat, football-shaped piece of compressed wood—called a biscuit—would fit into a pair of matching slots.

How to Structure a Biscuit Joint

1. Line the two wood pieces you are planning to join together up carefully on your bench. Use a pencil to mark where you will place the joints.

2. Once you have made the pencil marks, secure the wood to your bench or in a vice, so it is held steady for the cut. Manage your biscuit joiner for the size of the biscuits you will need for your project.

3. Cut into the wood on the marked lines.

4. Make sure your planks join together neatly and tight, then insert the wood biscuits and, while clamping the wood, bond the planks together. Note that the wood biscuits can be bought in hardware stores.

Biscuits

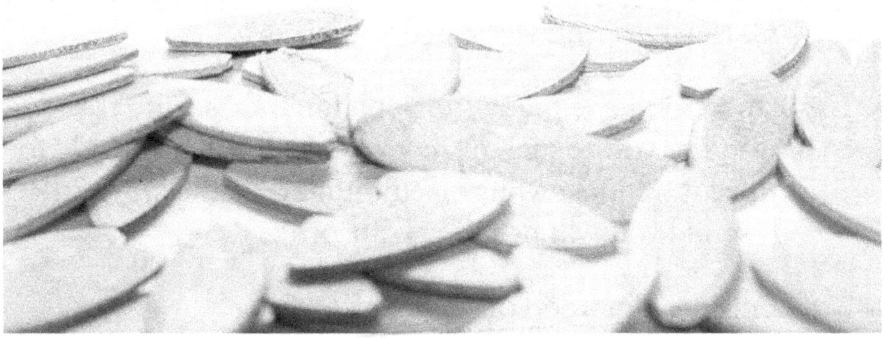

Three-way Joint (kawai tsugite)

Most joints are created with only one or two directions in mind. The *kawai tsugite* joint fits together perfectly in three ways. Assembling the *kawai tsugite* joint either goes as two corner joints or one straight one. At the intermediate skill level, it is important to have a grip on the principles detailed here, as it is one thing to understand how this joint works, but another one completely to cut it into a piece of timber. It is difficult enough to cut a rectangle or square into this new shape, let alone doing it well. The end result of crafting this joint is nice to look at, but due to how the joint reacts with the woodgrain, it is weaker than other types of joints detailed here. However, being at the intermediate skill level, one must know how to craft the *kawai tsugite*. There are different ways to assemble this joint; as mentioned earlier, either two corner joints or a straight joint. First, the tools you will need include:

- A perfect square of timber.
- A back saw.
- Chisel (skewed or straight).
- Marking gauge.
- Bevel gauge.
- Try-square.
- Miter-square.
- A pencil or marking knife.
- Vise
- Bench hook.
- A workbench.

Steps

1. Plane your square of wood to be entirely round. They have to be the exact same dimensions in thickness and in width. You can also cut one piece in half; that way, the grain will be the same for when they are put together in a straight line). Mark a perfect cubic square with a colored pencil (blue). Then, mark 45-degree lines from one corner to the other corner (red). Finally, mark the lines from the midpoint to the corner (green).

2. Along the 45-degree marking (from corner to corner), cut off the corner of the post.

3. Mark new lines on the cut face by connecting the points on each.
4. Using a saw to cut as much of the timber as possible. This will give a smooth face for chiseling. It will also save you a great deal of time.
5. After the cut, chisel out the remaining wood between the cut portions.
6. Put the pieces together. Note that the first try, you may find that you have to chisel a bit more to make them flush.

Dovetail Joint

At the intermediate skill level, you must become proficient in dovetailing, as it is an effective technique when it comes to joining boards together.

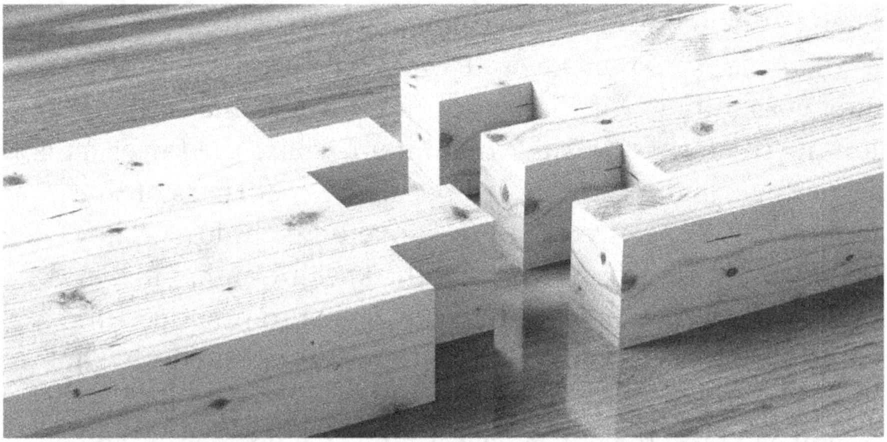

Dovetail joints, although beautifully crafted, are also somewhat complicated and created in the shape of a bird tail for a reason. These joints are known for their tensile strength, meaning that they are resistant to being pulled apart. Working dovetail joints are a sign that you have acquired true, intermediate Japenese joinery skills. Because they are free of mechanical joints, they are also much more pleasing to the eye. Important evidence to back up the stealthy nature of the dovetail joint can be observed in almost any antique shop. One need only open one of the drawers on an old desk to see a sure sign of their quality. Dovetail joints are the strongest joints in all of Japanese joinery and will hold together with or without glue. This is the perfect joint for any intermediate joiner to master, as the challenge in creating them lies in their difficulty to mark out and cut. If cut incorrectly, they will lose their advantages previously described. Making sure you design the right type of dovetail for your projects is crucial in building strength in the creation and paying noteage to your skill set and abilities.

The most common usage of this joint is in where the sides dresser drawers are joined. A series of "tails" cut from the end of one plank interlock with a series of "pins" that have been cut from another end of the plank. Together, they form a trapezoidal shape. Dovetail joints have been used in Japanese joinery for thousands of years as a method for joining the front and sides of an item. There are fewer nails, fastenings, and rivets needed because the corners of the joinery can be secured with the dovetail technique. They create cohesion by interlocking the specific cuts, pins, and tails needed to form it. It might be smart to practice with extra wood to see which technique suits you the best. That way, you can try different types of dovetail joints and avoid mistakes in the bigger project. Using the old-fashioned way to cut dovetails gives a unique, handcrafted appearance to your project. With patience and lots of practice, you can master the fulfilling skill of hand-cut dovetails.

The one disadvantage the dovetail has is in comparing it to a box joint. The dovetail joint has fewer tenons than a box joint and they do not go all the way through a piece of timber. In addition, dovetails are used for pulling away from a piece in one direction, whereas a box joint is strong in both directions.

Tools Needed for Dovetail Joints

- Chisel set.
- Marking knife.
- Dovetailing saw.

- Mallet.
- Square.
- Vise.

Cutting Dovetail Joints

With just a little practice, cutting dovetail joints can be fairly easy. Make sure your tools are maintained and ready; it doesn't matter how good your technique is if your tools are not ready for service. Secure your timber with your vice and mark how deep you will cut. You can use your marking gauge for this.

Mark your tails, from the end of the board to the top of the square and the face of the board, and the areas you will be removing. From where you've marked, cut out the tails. If need be, you can mark the cutting angle until you have a good feel with your saw. The following are steps for clearing out spare wood:

A. The best method for clearing out spare wood is by chiseling approximately 1/16th of an inch, as close as you can to the depth line.

B. Make a quick downstroke along the depth line. From there, make a 30-degree angle pair back to stop the most recent cut.

C. Continue this process until you're halfway, then flip your piece over. Keep cutting until you break through.

D. Chisel into the stop line to remove any extra wood. Continue all the way across the line.

E. Repeat this process at the halfway point, then flip your board over. Continue the process once more until you break through to the other side.

F. Mark the pins. Like with the tails, use a single board to cut the pins necessary for the formation of the dovetail joint.

G. Place the pin piece in your vise with the end sticking out about an ⅛th of an inch. Hold a block aligned to the projection of the face. Using a tail board, place the end of the tail piece in tight to the block and align the edges. While applying pressure, mark to the end of the pin board, like you did with the tail board.

H. Cut out the pins. Like the tails, your square will come in handy. Mark vertical lines for your cuts. Then, clean out any waste wood.

I. With your vise, rotate the pin board 90 degrees before you cut to the depth line. This will loosen debris from around the edge of the face. Clean any waste by chiseling, just the same as you did with the tail waste.

J. Fit the boards together (you may need to make some final chisels). Gently chisel any excess wood until you have a perfect fit. Make sure there are no gaps.

K. Now the boards, pins, and tails are set for a perfect fit. Apply some force and lock the boards, forming a corner.

Circle true or false: Intermediate skills include using dovetails of intersecting corners.

Finally, it is time to clean up. It is imperative that you clean off any waste, so it won't ruin your dovetail. A clean workplace ensures a smooth process from start to finish. Having less clutter around will also help you focus more. With this important step of cleaning, you are well on your way to successfully producing the type of dovetail corners you desire. Dovetails are strong joints that will stand the test of time.

Types of Dovetails

a. *Through dovetails*: The simplest and oldest type of dovetail used in joinery. When cut, two separate pieces of timber intersect, making a perfect corner that fits securely and firmly.

b. *Sliding dovetail joints*: Work with a long tail with carved grooves. These dovetails' sides are also angled, so it can adhere to a longboard pin that keeps it in place. Sliding dovetail joints are stronger than dado joints because they do not depend completely on glue. Also, the dovetail shoulders keep the edges of the slot hidden and pay tribute to the visible art of good craftsmanship.

c. *Box-joint dovetails*: Use simple straight cuts for pins and tails, but can be less durable.

Box Dovetails

1. The difference between a *dovetail* and a *box dovetail* is that the digits on the box dovetail are rectangular rather than shaped like a dove's tail. There are different ways to cut box-joint dovetails; for example, you can do it with a chisel and a dovetail saw by

deciding on a width for the fingers, which would divide uniformly into the width of the wood for the project. So, if your wood's width is 6 inches, a ½-inch wide finger would make 12 in total, 6 for each piece of wood. You can also cut them by machine if you do not want to take the time to cut them by hand. Almost all dovetail jigs cut box joints. Look at the documentation that came with your jig—it should describe the process as the same as cutting the tails of a regular dovetail joint, but using a straight cutting bit instead of a dovetail bit. An even easier way is to use your table saw with an arranged dado set. The cut depth should be the same height as the wood's thickness.

2. Adhere a piece of scrap wood to your miter gauge. Make sure it is wide enough so that when connected to the miter gauge, it extends past the blade by an inch, and 2 inches past the miter gauge on the left side.

3. Make sure the scrap wood is square to the blade, then pass the scrap wood through the saw.

4. Move the piece of scrap wood to the right by twice the width of the fingers after removing it from the gauge, then reattach it to the miter gauge.

5. Cut one small piece of wood the same width as the fingers, which will connect into the cut made in the scrap. Note that this piece should be two times as wide as the piece you are working with.

6. Adhere this piece into the notch you made in the scrap using a wood screw from the bottom, and make it so that it sticks forward from the scrap toward the blade of the saw. This will be your finger cutting gauge.

7. Make sure the miter is square to the blade and make a new notch in the current position on the scrap wood.

8. Now you have made the jig. Take one of the pieces you are working with and place it firmly against the scrap on the end, up to the small guide you attached to the notch in your scrap piece.

9. Hole the wood firmly against the scrap piece and guide it through the saw. Once clear, run the whole assembly back through the blade. Now you have your first notch and finger at precisely the right width. Continue this process until all fingers for your project have been formed.

10. The opposing piece of wood is cut much in the same way, except the initial cut is not made with the wood against the guide. The outside edge of the opposing piece should be even with the dado blade's outside edge. This is easily positioned by aligning the outer edge of the wood piece with the edge of the notch in the scrap piece. Once you have lined it up, make an initial cut, continuing until complete.

11. Once both sides of the joint's fingers are formed, dry fit the joint.

12. Next, put a thin layer of flue on the surface of all of the joints, then guide them together and clam if necessary. This technique is fine for crafting drawers or making boxes. Note that you should be diligent when it comes to clamping the box square.

The box joint is a relatively strong and useful joint that can be a lot of fun to build. It is not as elegant as dovetails, but certainly very appropriate in some circumstances.

Half-blind Dovetails

This cut realizes only one visible dovetail joint, which is not the best for large furniture. It is a joint that does a superb job in its strength and beauty without begging for attention; this is the nature of the half-blind dovetail on a well-made dresser drawer. This is for the intermediate crafter and one who has mastered all other dovetails. The half-blind dovetail is cut the same way, with the difference being that half-blind pins need careful sawing and additional chiseling. The following are steps for a dresser drawer, which you will be making as one of the projects in this book.

1. Cut the groove for the bottom of the drawer in the front and sides. Note that once the joint is assembled, you will be unable to see the ends of the tails. All the groves in the sides of the drawers can be sawed all the way through.

2. Next, you have to decide how long the tails will be (how near they come to the drawer front's exterior). For drawers that are 3/4 inches thick on the front, make the tails approximately 5/8 inches long, but leave a 1/8-inch lap. If you make the lap of the joint much thicker, it will look awkward. If you make it too thin, you might chisel through it when you are cutting the sockets for the tails. It is a 5 to 1 ratio.

3. Put the marking gauge edge up against the inside face of the drawer front and adjust your cutter by leaving a 1/8-inch lap. Place a mark on the drawer front's ends. Then, run the gauge's fence—leaving it at the same setting—along the edge front of the side of each drawer, marking the faces on the inside and outside.

4. Reset the gauge to the thickness of the sides and draw a line on the drawer at each end (front and inside). Set the gauge with a cutter just overhanging the side, so the pins will be a bit longer than the side is thick. That way, they will be easier to sand or plane flush after assembly.

5. Lay out the tails on the side of the drawers and cut them the same way as you do for through-dovetail joints.

6. Reset the gauge to the thickness of the sides and scribe a line on each end of the drawer front, on the inside face. When I set the gauge for this line, I let the cutter overhang the side; that way, the pins will be slightly longer than the side is thick, and they'll be easy to plane or sand flush after assembly. With the marking gauge work finished, lay out the tails on the drawer sides and cut them, just as you would for through-dovetail joints.

Mitered Dovetail Joint (kakushi arigata kumitsugi)

The mitered dovetail joint is also referred to as the secret miter dovetail joint—the pins and tails on this joint are hidden and when assembled, it appears as a miter joint. This type of joint is used primarily because of its strength, since when it is finished, it will have the appearance of a miter joint but the strength of something bigger. The following are items you'll need and steps to take in order to make one.

1. Two pieces of 6-inch wide pine (it has a straight grain and is not too difficult to work with). Be sure there are no knots where you will be cutting the pins and tails.

2. Set a wheel marking gauge to the thickness of the timber.
3. Use another wheel marking gauge set to 3/16 inches.
4. Lay out your timber so you can match the grain and label the inside and outside.
5. Use a marking gauge set to the thickness of the timber and draw lines on the interior of each piece.
6. Use a marking gauge set at 3/16 inch and draw a line on the interior of each piece.
7. With the same marking gauge, draw a line on each plank at the end, off of the outside (this is where the rabbet will be cut).
8. Mark the line around the sides (outline the rabbet).
9. Here lies the challenge—using a miter saw, set so it won't cut all the way through the plank. To do this, adjust the miter so it leaves 3/16 inch of the rabbet's bottom. The cut has to be neat and accurate.
10. This can also be done with a hand saw or miter gauge and table saw. If the saw's blade doesn't make the bottom flat, don't cut it all the way to the scrib. Clean the bottom up with your chisel or router plane (see image below).

Cross Lap Joint

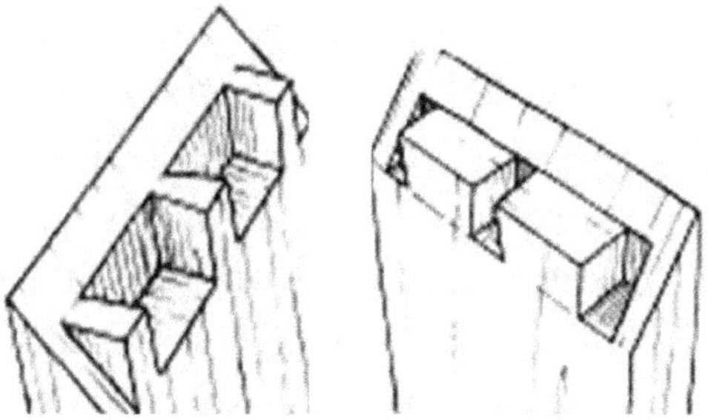

A lap joint can either be a full lap or half lap joint. With a full lap joint, none of the material is taken from each of the pieces that are to be joined, resulting in a joint that is the thickness of two pieces. With a half lap joint, material is taken out from both pieces, so the end result is the thickness of the thickest piece.

In Japanese joinery, a cross lap joint is when glue joins two long-grain timber faces. It is one of the strongest in its ability to defend shar forces—more than even mortise, tenon, and other well-known "strong" joints. Also referred to as overlapping joints, cross lap joints are used to design continuous, beautiful lines in furniture. Cross lap joints are akin to what you would see in the joinery of log cabins. Each log of timber interlocks neatly to the next without the need for adhesive or nails. However, you want to use nuts and bolts for additional reinforcement.

The edges of cross lap joints are completely level with the surface. Knowing how to achieve cross lap joints in joinery is imperative for making frames or furniture. You will need to take out a section of wood from each adjoining wood piece, and then clamp them together. The difference between a cross lap and half lap is that the joint sits in the middle of either one or both pieces, rather than at the end. The two pieces are at 90-degree angles to each other, and one piece may stop at the joint or carry on past it. When one piece stops at the shin, it is called a middle or "tee" lap. In the cross lap, when both pieces go beyond the joint, both pieces have two shoulders and one cheek. This joint is commonly used for framing cabinets and for bracing items.

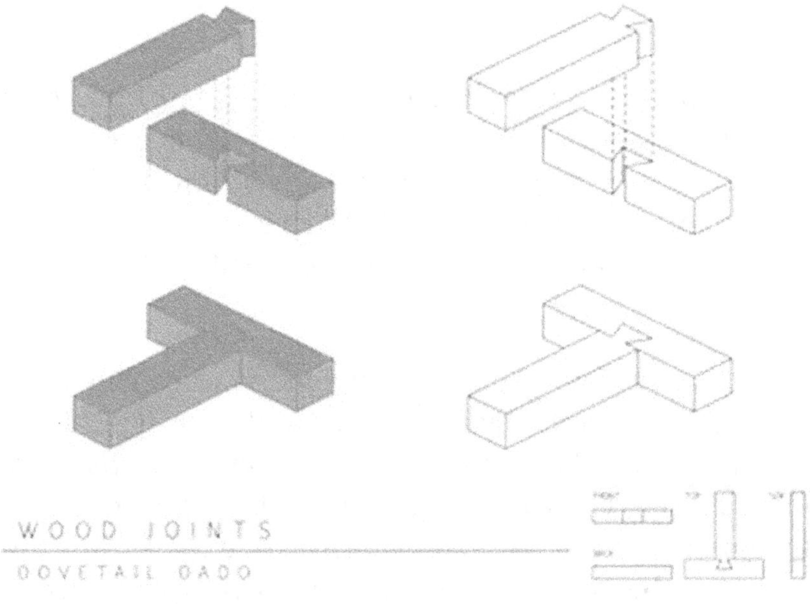

Tools Needed:

- Table saw.
- Router.

- Jigs.
- Marking gauge.

Steps

1. **Square lines**—With your knife, face mark and square the pieces.
2. **Square**—With the upper parts against the squares, lay the pieces on each other by taking off the square and pencil marking the points at the sides for width.
3. At the marked points, square a line across your timber on both of the pieces of wood making sure to mark halfway across the edges.
4. Set the marking gauge for one-half of the woods' thickness.
5. **Saw**—Chisel a V-shaped groove to start the sawing process and run your saw against the line, making sure the cut is accurate.
6. **Wood waste**—Remove excess wood by making a couple of cuts, and then chisel.

Isuka-Tsugi (crossbill joint)

The crossbill joint (*isuka-tsugi*) is used to secure a horizontal piece of wood to the face of a square pillar. It is called a crossbill joint because it looks like a bird's bill. Make cuts on two corners of the same side of the pillar, leaving the center section uncut. The horizontal beam has a single notch cut so it can be hammered into the flat center part between the two notched corners until secured. The uncut part fits into the gaps in the corner.

Isuzaka Shachi (Crossbill + Shachi)

Shachi is a thin peg inserted into a hole where it will receive the corresponding tenon (projecting piece). This technique strengthens the joint. In Japanese joinery, there are two very different types: crossbill joints and scarf joints. The type depends on whether the joint's face interlocks or not. An ordinary scarf joint is just two flat pieces connecting on an angle relative to the axis of the piece being joined. It depends wholly on the glue and/or screws, bolts, and nails. Interlocking crossbill joints vary depending on the degree of tension and compression strength, but most crossbill joints need mechanical tools to keep them closed. A plain scarf joint is not the joint of choice when strength is needed, so it is used more for decorations. However, with the advent of "super glues," the structural performance of a plain scarf joint has been enhanced.

The joint is made by cutting opposite tapered ends on each piece when they are connected together. For crafters, this makes for a better long-grain to long-grain surface to glue, which makes a stronger joint than one could achieve through crafting a simple butt joint. The tapers are usually cut at an angle ratio of about 1:10. The plain scarf's ends are separated by tiny lines to a fine point, which helps hide the joint of the finished project. By contrast in other scarf forms, the ends are frequently cut to a blunt nib, which connects to a matching shoulder of the partnering piece.

A crossbill joint can also be used to mend problems made when a plank has been cut too short for the project. The plank can be halved with a tapered cut, then make a scarf joint. When the joint is glued together, the tapers slide against one another making it so the two pieces are not any longer in line with one another. This, in effect, can make a longer board. Once the glue dries, the plank can be sanded down to an even thickness, meaning it's thinner but longer.

Koshikake-Ari-Tsugi (half-lap dovetail joint)

Shaped much like a trapezoid, the half-lap dovetail joint used to couple horizontal pieces. This combines two joints, a half-lap and a dovetail, making an end joint. The dovetail hole and the bench part of the Japanese joint are cut so the hole is approximately half the thickness of the wood. The seat or bench made from the half that remains sticks out like a step beyond the hold.

The second piece of wood has the dovetail projecting piece. Here, the undercut extends over to cover the bench partially when the dovetail projection is placed into the corresponding hold. This makes a face-grain-to-face-grain joint with lots of surface to glue. Butt joints differ, in that they depend on end-grain-to-end-grain connectedness that can break easily. Even if a butt joint is reinforced with a dowel, they are still not as strong as a half-lap dovetail joint.

This provides a face-grain-to-face-grain joint with plenty of gluing surface. Simple butt joints, on the other hand, rely on an end-grain-to-end-grain bond that can break easily. Even a dowel-reinforced butt joint won't prove as strong as a half-lap. Half-laps are commonly used for outdoor furniture, dressers (internal pieces), leg frames, and even your shop-cabinet door frames. You only need a radial-arm or table saw to craft a half-lap joint. For faster and smoother results, you can also use a dado set. However, if you don't have one that will cut cross grain cleanly and leave the surface flat and smooth where you sawed, you should use a router table equipped with a straight bit.

Steps

1. Install your dado to 13/16 inches, so you can achieve the widest possible cut.

2. Calibrate your rip fence, where one edge of your wood piece bumps against the fence and the opposing edge aligns with the dado side calibrated farthest from the fence.

3. You can keep your fence calibrated to this position for the rest of the cuts, provided all of the pieces are the same width. If they are different widths, note that you can use a piece of another adjoining piece to calibrate the fence for the half-lap cut (i.e. horizontal pieces are used for a door frame to calibrate the fence for the cuts in the vertical pieces, and vice versa).

4. Calibrate the cutting depth of the dado unit to where it takes off exactly half of the wood piece thickness. Use some scrap wood to test cutting depth that is of the same thickness as your work pieces. Note that after you cut the scrap wood, you need to place them on a flat surface and line them up so the top and bottom faces are smooth together.

5. Place a mark on the face side of your wood pieces, so as to not confuse them. Note that you will have to place the face side of one piece and the face side of the connecting piece down.

6. Attach an additional wooden fence to your miter gauge, which should be calibrated for a square cut. The added piece should be with a ½ inch of the touching side against the rip fence.

7. Place the wood pieces in position, with an edge up against the added fence and one end pushed against the rip fence.

8. Holding the wood piece firmly against the added fence, pass the piece through the dado set, making consecutive passes until you finish the half-lap cut.

9. Apply wood glue to all of the surfaces to be matted. Bring the wood pieces together with bar or pipe clamps.

10. Put the glued surfaces together tightly with a smaller clamp. To clamp the joint, first apply wood glue to all mating surfaces. Draw the workpieces together with bar or pipe clamps. Then, bring the glued surfaces tightly together with a small clamp.

11. On the faces of the joints, put a piece of scrap wood on, so they are protected from the jaws of the clamp.

12. Every so often, you need to put a half-lap joint on the piece somewhere other than the end. All you would do is mark with a pencil the overlap position onto the piece's edge. The piece will be cut in its center section.

13. Calibrate the edge of the unmarked piece against the additional fence of the miter-gauge. Line up the pencil marks with the dado set sides and put two clamps (handscrew if possible, which is used for fastening a small piece on the drill press) on them. If you do not have handscrew clamps, just clamp together two wood blocks with bar clamps. If you have them situated correctly, the stops will restrict the area of wood that

has been removed from the space between your marks.

14. Align the other end of the wood pieces against the stop that remains and cut another one.

15. Remove all the wood material in between the two cuts. Now that you have your stops set up correctly, your pieces will all turn out to be the same.

Shiho-Kanawa (all-direction iron ring)

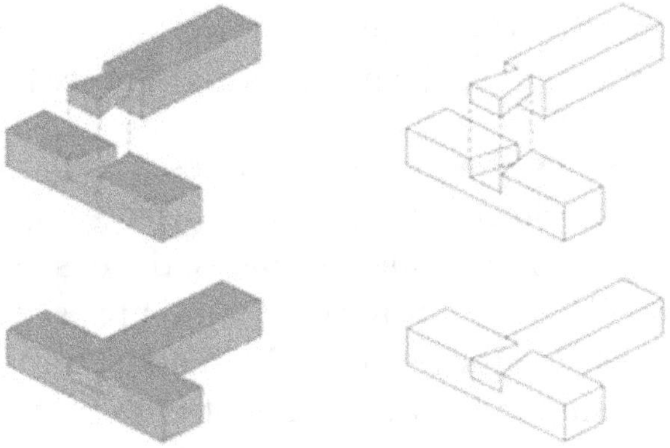

The *shiho-kanawa* is a mortised, rabbeted, oblique scarf joint, able to withstand weight from all directions. This is a notched cut on the end of the board that can support weight from all directions. It should be noted that this all-direction iron ring is a bit strange, in that it is hard to tell which direction it has been inserted from. It is configured by inserting the joint diagonally.

Both ends of the joints are the same and labeled upper and lower wood. Two holes are made deeper through inserting draw pins through the depth of the splice. The joint is crafted by moving the inside face of the upper wood over the inside face of the lower wood while keeping the surfaces of the middle face in close contact. The wood pieces are then secured together by two draw pins, successfully interlocking the back and front surfaces of the joint. The pins are put in from the thicker end toward the thinner one, alternating the process.

Shikake-Ari (locked dovetail joint)

The locked dovetail joint has a projecting tenon partially removed. This area is where the other section is secured with a dovetail joint, which is usually reinforced by combining it with other joints, so it can bear the stress of other loads.

When connecting squared wood pieces, you want the joints to be strong. Strength is acquired by crafting varying squared wood pieces, so if one dissipates, the design can remain strong. The use of ironware commonly used in carpentry today bears the burden of potential corrosion and coming loose as the timber ages. All matter decays with age; however, the decayed area can be removed and replaced with a new section. For this reason, Japanese joinery structures are some of the world's longest-lasting ones too.

Shiho-Henkei (omnidirectionally transformed joint)

Timber is alive and should be used in such a way that helps preserve its strength and natural beauty for as long as possible. This all-direction joint utilizes a differing joint on each side. When it is transformed, it is hard to tell how it has been connected.

Chapter Three: Project 1—Simple Stool

There is great satisfaction in creating something and completely bypassing the furniture stores. With your Japanese joinery tools in hand, you can be the master of your imagination. You can spend $50 on the materials you need for a piece of furniture that could cost upward of $500 to buy from a store. But remember, as with any applied skill, much of that success comes through trial and error. Wood will not forgive you for any mistakes made, so think carefully about each step and before you start a project. Think of the following saying: "Consider your timber species and ask yourself if pounding a nail into your 2 x 4, will it crack?" Have you practiced sanding enough to learn what affect the varying grits have on different surfaces?

The most essential aspect of Japanese joinery is patience and enjoyment. Focus on that as much or even more than the end result. If you focus on patience and enjoyment, you will go from intermediate to advanced woodcrafter before you know it. With all the projects set forth in this guide, you will be taking measurements. Here is a tip: stick a roll of masking tape in your toolkit or pocket and jot your measurements on the tape. Then, tear it off and stick it where it belongs on your project (stool, chair, table, dresser, shelves, etc.). Something as simple as this can make the experience so much more enjoyable.

Whichever project you are working on, remember that if you measure twice, you will only have to cut once! You will be starting with a simple stool, and as the projects proceed, they will gradually get a bit tougher as you gain more experience in your craft. Let's get started!

Materials:

1. 2 x 2 at 8 feet long (1).
2. 1 x 2 at 10 feet long (1).
3. 1 x 12 at 11½ inches long, or plywood around 12 inches long and ¾ inches thick. (1).
4. 1¼-inch pocket hole screws.
5. Sandpaper.
6. Wood filler.
7. Wood glue.
8. Stain.

What to Cut:

1. (4) 2 x 2 at 23¼ inches long, cut ends at a 5-degree angle and bevel(4) 1 x 2 at 7 inches (short point to short point) cut ends at a 5-degree angle. They are not parallel.
2. (2) 1 x 2 at 10 inches cut same as above. They are not parallel.
3. (2) 1 x 2 at 8¼ inches; same as above.
4. (2) 1 x 2 at 9½ inches; cut same as above.
5. (2) 1 x 2 at 8 inches; cut same as above.

6. (1)1 x 12 at 11½ inches; make the cut to a square by measuring the width of your 1 x 12.

Steps

1. Set your saw to a 5-degree angle and a 5-degree bevel. Trim as close to the end of the 2 x 2 as possible.
2. Measure 23¼ inches and make a cut along the same edge. Now you have one leg.
3. Do the same by sliding the board down as you make more cuts until you have all four cuts out of the 8-foot long 2 x 2.
4. All ends are to be cut at the 5-degree angle for the rungs and supports (no bevel). Different from the legs, the ends will *not* be parallel.
5. Make a 5-degree cut, rotate your board 180 degrees (like you are rolling a rolling pin) and measure your cut from short point to short point.
6. Make another 5-degree cut.
7. Mark the inside corners of the legs, noting that these corners are on the inside (so you don't lose track of the correct leg positions).
8. Cut four top supports at 7 inches long, with both ends at 5-degree angles (not parallel; short point to short point).
9. Attach two legs to the top support.
10. Using pocket holes, build two of these. Center your top supports.

11. Add additional rungs for support.
12. Connect the two leg frames to the remaining top supports.
13. Connect the top by screwing through the top supports to the bottom side of the top, so you hide the screw holes.
14. Use wood filler to fill the holes and let dry.
15. Using 120 grit sandpaper around the top until it is comfortable to sit on.
16. Finally, flip it over and burnish to match your dining room.

Chapter Four:
Project 2—Three-Shelved Rack

Design your own three-shelved rack and base it on your available space. When making your shelves, measure the space available; don't go thinking that all areas are square. You will want to add some vertical sections every 30 inches and give or pulse so your shelving doesn't sag. For a normal, 1-inch wood piece, do not use more than 18 to 24-inch spans.

You can return and cut 1-inch square side panels and place them vertically on the lower shelf for added support if need be. Crafting your own shelves is a wise investment. Using your Japanese joinery skills will return furniture that will appreciate in value with time, due to its high quality. By creating your own shelves, you will have a piece of craftsmanship that will maintain its beauty and value as an inspired work of art constructed by your own hands. Building shelves are one of the most common joinery projects. Building shelves that need to support a substantial amount of weight to stack books or even hold an audio system can be a bit tricky. Using a 1-inch thick piece of plywood will most likely sag in the middle under a considerable amount of weight.

Three-shelved rack

Materials:

1. 1 x 12-inch timber. Have your measurements for the outer box, shelves, and vertical supports. Note that timber comes in 96-inch sections, so you will have some scrap left over.

2. Poplar or maple wood; other species have knots, making them harder to work with.

3. 1 x 2-inch supporting strips, multiplied by the length of your shelves.
4. 1/8-inch plywood for the back.
5. Four supporting pins for each shelf.
6. Wood or drywall screws.
7. Small wire brads for mounting the back.

Steps:

1. Measure the wood cut to fit the shape of the basse box. As a top, you can add or subtract the wood's width, depending on which way your joints lap.
2. Put the box together and place on the plywood backing.
3. Measure every vertical section again, and then cut.
4. Drill the holes necessary for the project.
5. Prior to mounting the vertical box sections, cut dados to mount in the shelves.
6. Take measurements of the pin diameter.
7. Drill the necessary holes. Before mounting the vertical sections in the box, either drill holes for the supporting pins or cut grooves (dados) to mount the shelves into. Using a caliper with a size fitting the diameter of the pins and choose a bit for a loose fit (use scrap for trial and error).

8. Drill perpendicular to the wood holes. As an added tip, you can use a template for hole marking.

9. Stage the vertical sections.

10. Double check the joints to make sure they are square.

11. Measure the length of each shelf and cut.

12. Insert the pins for a test fit.

13. Take out the shelves and add a 1 x 2 inch supporting strip up front for added support.

14. Put the shelves back in.

15. Use 1½ strips of wood along the sides, top, and vertical supports if you want to cover the joint work.

Option 2: Breadboard Edge

- Flatten one side of the board with your plane. First, shave the raised spots, then plan from one end to the other.

- After you have figured out how long you want your shelves to be, the breadboard ends would be about 2-3 inches wide. You can make them wider or narrower if you wish. Then, make the mortise (hole) about ⅔ the width of the end piece.

- Cut the tongue (protruding side) approximately ¼ narrower than the length of the mortise in the end piece. Next, drill the peg holes through the middle of the protruding end piece (tongue) length.

- The length of the ends will equal the width of the wood panel at its widest (to account for humidity). If you are in a cold and dry environment, make the breadboard ends a bit longer than the width of the wood panel.

- Mortise the end sections.

  a. Center a ¼-inch mortise (cut a hole) 2⅛ inches deep on one edge of each end piece. Make sure to stop ¾ inches from the end. Drill the holes at both ends first, then drill evenly spaced holes in between each end.

  b. Clean the holes out.

  c. Create overlapping holes with a drill, beginning at the ends. Afterward, make the sides and ends straight and smooth with a chisel and square the corners.

  d. Center a ¼-inch projection strip (tongue) 2 inches long on each end of the board.

  e. Using a guide block to keep the saw in line and cut the laid-out shoulders crafting the tongue width at ¼ inches. Lay out and cut the shoulders to make the tongue width a ¼ inch less than the mortise length.

  f. Assemble the end pieces, centering on the board width. One inch from the joint, along a line, drill ¼-inch holes ⅝ inches deep in the center and 2¾ inches from each end.

Chapter Five: Project 3—Cupboard with Two Shelves

Making your own cupboard will give you the ability to personalize your work to what you want. The quality of your cupboard will depend on the quality of your materials. Since you are crafting it yourself, your cupboard will meet your specifications and should have a higher quality of wood. Customize your cupboard to fit your design style, storage inclination, and lifestyle. By deciding on the design that will go into your cupboard yourself, it becomes an even better representation of you.

Step 1: (*see diagram below*)

The body of this cupboard is crafted with ¾-inch plywood.

A. Cut each long side.

B. Cut the bottom and middle shelves.

C. Before attaching, add your shelf pin holes to the sides.

D. Adhere the shelf boards to the sides with mortise and tenon.

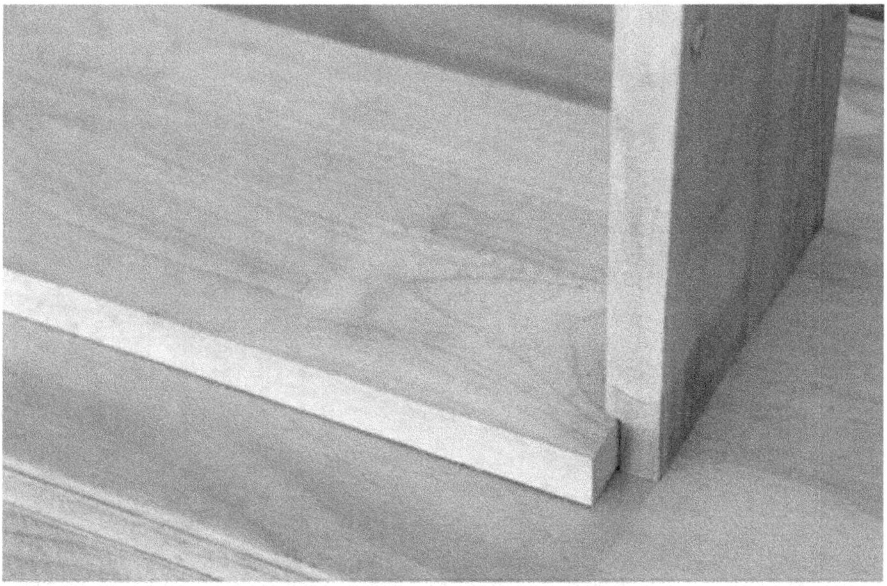

shutterstock.com • 748731829

Step 2:

A. Adhere the back support plank to the top and the back of the cupboard. This plank attaches the cupboard to the wall when finished.

B. Make sure to mark which side of the line you will set your mortise.

C. Adhere this plank to the side boards' mortise and tenon.

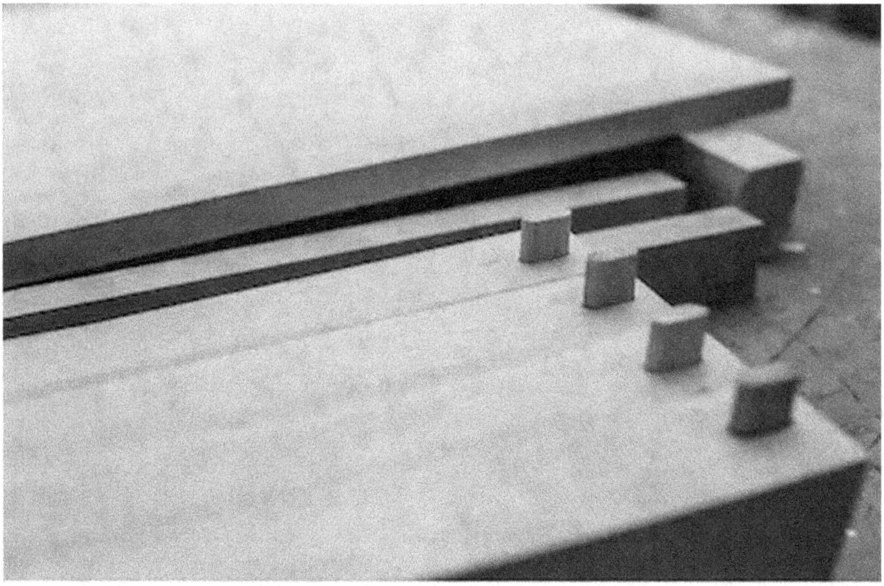

Step 3:

A. Build the frame face.

B. The top and side planks are 1 x 3, and the bottom board is 1 x 4.

C. Mortise holes on the bottoms and tenons on the tops of the side boards.

D. Connect all the planks to construct the frame.

Step 4:

A. Connect the frame face to the front of the cupboard.

B. Place your mortise and tenon on the inside of the cupboard and through the frame face.

C. The frame face must be flush against the sides and top of the cupboard.

Step 5:

A. Check that the following is true, and note the details:

a. The door back is ½-inch hardwood plywood. Note that hardwood plywood has a front and back.

b. Hardwood plywood has a face and back decorative covering made of hardwood instead of softwood like cedar or pine. It is stronger than solid wood and comes in varying species.

c. The door back is ½-inch hardwood plywood.

d. The back of the door is ½-inch hardwood plywood.

e. The front trim on the door is referred to as the "bender board. Note that the bender board is specifically good at fitting tight corners.

f. If you do not have a bender board, use ¼-inch craft boards for the trim.

Step 6:

A. Saw the horizontal and vertical planks first, then cut to size and attach them with ⅝-inch brad nails.

Step 7:

A. Saw the diagonal boards to 1½ inches wide each. Mark them with a pencil to fit beforehand.

B. Attach them with ⅝-inch brad nails and glue.

Step 8:

A. The cupboard top is an edge-glued panel. Note that wood pieces glued along their edges to create products of greater width.

B. Adhere the top. After that, taper all the shelf supports. For the "tapering jig," you can just use a 2x4 clamped at a slight angle to the table saw sled. Drill a hole near the end to clamp it and cut the end of the 2x4 at the appropriate angle.

C. Using a push stick, hold down the wood and cut it.

D. Taper the shelf supports. Tapering jig is a 2 x 4 clamped at an angle to the sled of the table saw, with a drilled hole by the end to clamp. Then, cut the end of the 2 x 4 at the appropriate angle.

E. Use a push stick while you cut to hold down the wood.

F. Edge-glued panels usually come ready to varnish.

Step 9:

A. The cupboard back is ¼-inch hardwood plywood.

B. Cut the cupboard back to size and adhere it to the back using ¾-inch brad nails or staples.

Step 10:

A. The shelf planks will all be crafted with ¾-inch hardwood plywood. Make three.

B. Adhere the shelves using glue on both the mortise and tenon underneath each shelf plank. If you have shelf pin holes, make the planks a ¼ inch shorter, so there is room for the shelf pins on each side.

C. Craft the drawer supports. Using ¾-inch plywood and a table saw, cut to size.

D. Connect the top board mortise, then adhere them to the side tenons using wood glue.

E. Connect the mortise and tenons of the bottom and top of the vertical plank.

F. Do the same thing on the opposing side of the cupboard. Note that these are the planks your drawer slides will be attached to.

Step 11:

A. At last, craft your drawers.

B. Use a ¾-inch plywood for all sides of the drawers. Note that you can also use 1 x 4 planks.

C. Adhere each corner using 1¼-inch brad nails and wood glue.

D. Each drawer has a base plywood of ½ inch.

E. Using wood glue and 1¼ brad nails, attach it to the box.

Chapter Six: Project 4—Dining Table and Chairs

You have already made a dining table in the beginners' guide and chair in this book's first project. The unit of dining table and chairs is essential to understand scale and proportion. Making one object is easy, but making more in reference and correspondence to each other needs strong imagination.

Make a detailed sketch of your unit. If possible, you can use a computer-based software to create a 3D model that will help you view your ideal image and placement in a room. You can make it dynamic and contemporary in terms of design. You can also add a stool for seating arrangements for a kid.

If you are enjoying quality entertainment and dining with friends and family in your home, your dining room needs to have a comfortable atmosphere. Unfortunately, if the furniture is cramped or the chairs make people fidget during a meal, you will basically be unsatisfied. Sometimes, the dimensions of a dining room can be too limited, or the chairs are a hindrance. If so, it is time to put your intermediate skills of Japanese joinery to work. Maybe the shuffle to buy a new dining set seemed unappealing to your personal taste. Rather than acquiesce and buy something to "make do" or just have something new, you can set off on a new adventure in Japanese joinery. Follow the directions in this chapter to create a new and beautiful dining room table and chairs.

Many people think crafting your own furniture is solely for the wealthy; however, this quality furniture will not need replacing, and it will give you the chance to have a perfect fit. Your uniqueness will make a clear statement. You will know it was crafted with care and has long-term durability, giving you a high return on your investment. By commissioning your own dining room set, you will create an air of sentimentality for the whole family and all your friends, on top of it being a great conversational piece.

Selecting the Species of Wood

Mixing together different tones of wood is perfectly acceptable. However, as a starting point, pick a dominant tone to help you decide on other pieces to compliment the environment. For instance, if your floors are wooden, that would be the dominant tone. If you do not have a wooden floor, pick a dominant tone that matches the largest piece of furniture in the room. The creative goal here is continuity. Try to tell a story by noticing fine details, such as wood grain, undertones, and finish.

Match undertones: For example, many pieces of antique wood are in a warm mid-tone. Notice your dominant wood tone to see if it is warmer or cooler, and then try to continue that tone.

Playing with contrast: While it may seem contrary, mixing tones of wood is encouraged. Lightly colored floors may be complemented by a dark toned coffee table. Contrasting tones adds visual regard and provides more depth.

The finish: If you have mixed tones, you can show progression by using similar finishes. For instance, if you have a glossy floor or dining room table, follow suit with matching chairs that have a glossy finish.

Texture: Using different types of wood for furnishings does not simply mean to choose different wood stains or species of wood. It can also mean paying attention to the texture of the wood. Wood can be rough, smooth, knotty, weathered, or polished. Using wood with different textures can make for an interesting contrast in your decor. If your wooden floors are smooth, you may liven things up with a table you crafted with hand-scraped designs. Or you may compliment your smooth wooden floors with a knotty pine desk. As a tip, there can be such a thing as overkill when choosing your wood designs. It is best to stick to no more than a few different types of wood.

Accents: Breaking up your wood components with a nice rug can have a significant impact, especially if your wood tones are all the same. For example, if all of you have washed-out wood tones throughout the room, an area rug with deep colors will compliment your furniture.

Ahead of your project, place tape on your floor to see the size you would like for your table. Then, lay out the materials you are going to use to build the table, making sure you have the side you want to eat on face down (you are building it upside down).

Step 1 - The Shape you want

A. Decide if you want rectangular, oval, round, or square taking into account the shape of your dining room.

Step 2 - Material Selection

A. 4 X 8 Foot sheet of plywood ¾ inch plywood. Easy to cut and round of edges or corners. For a normal family size table.

B. Material *for legs*

a. 2x4s

b. Glue

c. Clamps

d. Drill & countersink bit

e. Wood filler

f. Table Saw

g. Sander

h. Sandpaper 120 grit

Wooden chairs are beautiful and timeless, as long as they are crafted to be comfortable. The chair needs to flex when sat upon. This chapter will step-by-step instruct the readers about a simple chair's function. The backrest is the most important feature of the chair. Most of all you will have a completely customized look for less than a fraction of the cost it would be to have one made. This chair will add a uniqueness to your home so you can avoid a generic looking style. You can take pride in knowing it is a one of a kind chair, not one a neighbor can come and see and then run out to buy. In this chapter the size, angle, proportions, and measurements will be covered along with discussions about the process, the angles, and various joints necessary to work the fittings. Finally, the importance of staining to give a finished look will be discussed. Crafting your own chairs puts the power of good quality and the look of costly finishes in quality furniture much less expensively than you would be at a store. By building your own furniture, you can add more support than anything you can find in a store. Also, your chairs will be made of 'real' wood which is made to stand the test of time. Choosing the right materials for your craft will determine its test of time. Knowing your own handiwork allows you to easily modify or fix something later.

Step 3 -Chairs

Construct the legs

A. Start with cutting the 2x4s to length and apply plenty of glue to the front of one of the 2×4 pieces.

B. Place the other 2×4 on top and move it around to create a suction to keep the top piece from sliding. Clamp them together until dry.

C. Before heading to the router table, lay out the mortise locations on the workpieces, but mark on the faces opposite where the mortises will go. This way you can see the marks as you rout the mortised face.

   a. Make a simple box to how the wood bar vertically for when you route the tenon in the head.

   b. On the box top but an inlay board with a holed to guide the router and shape the tenon.

   c. Decide the width of your mortises and tenons.

   d. The tenon should be ½ the length of the short side of the wood bar section.

   e. Your router bit diameter should be of equal length.

   f. Use the same router bit to make the mortises and tenons.

g. the mortise hole

h. the tenon tongue.

i. The tenon rail will fit into the hole you cut in the corresponding piece. Make sure to cut the tenon to fit your mortise hole exactly.

j. The mortise has shoulders that seat the joints as it completely enters the hole of the mortise.

D. For square legs use the table saw with the blade as far raised as possible.

E. Run each leg through twice with the rip fence set at 3-14 inches from the blade.

F. Sand out all milling marks, scratches, transition marks from the manufacturing process.

G. Trim the other side of the leg assemblies with the rip fence on the saw set at 3 inches.

H. Attach them underneath the table using screws and wood glue.

As a side note, if you would like to have a less formal dining room table instead, you can use large cable reels. They are the perfect height and strong enough to support the table. You can usually get them for free. Get two 29 inch reels and simply rest your table on top or coat with glue and attach your table top.

Design a few sketches before you start. Understand the measurement and purpose.

Chair dimensions

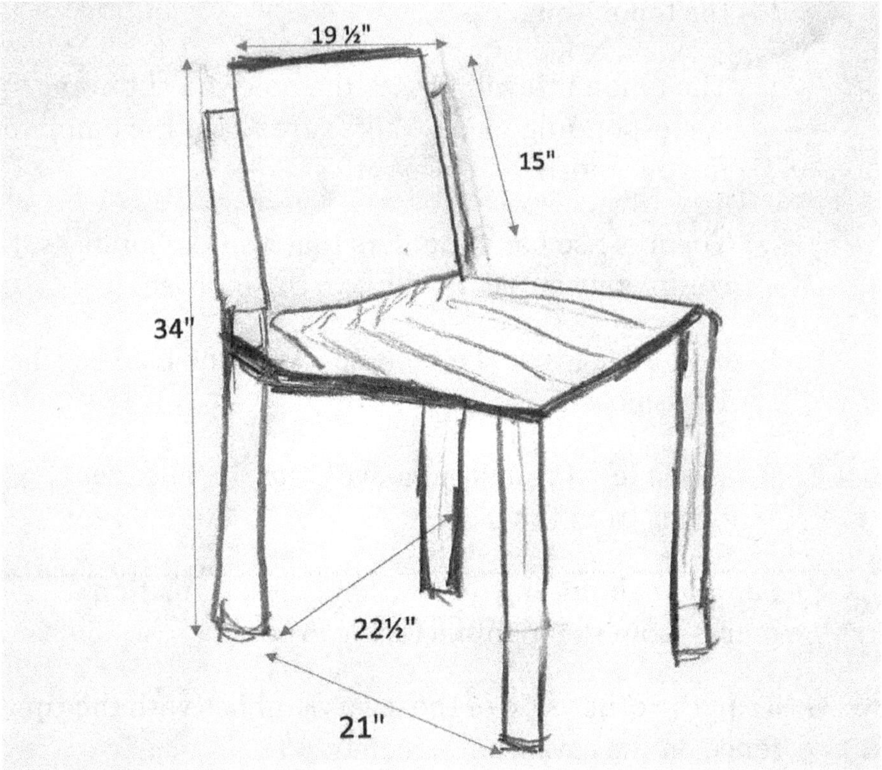

Materials:

1. 1x2″ 8ft. 1 piece.
2. 2x2″ 8ft. 2 pieces.
3. 2x4″ 8ft.1 piece.
4. 1x10″ 36in. 1 piece.
5. 3/8″ dowel rod 1 piece.
6. Wood glue.

7. Wood filler.

8. 120 grit sandpaper.

9. Primer.

10. Wood conditioner.

11. Outdoor wood finish.

Wood Cuts:

1. 2 – 2×4 at 30″; Cut the back of the chair.

2. 2 – 2×2 @ 19 1/2″; Cut the supports for the chair back.

3. 2 – 2×2 @ 18″; Cut the front legs.

4. 2 – 1×3 @ 17 1/2″; Cut the side apron.

5. 1 – 1×3 @ 16 1/2″; Cut the front apron.

6. 1 – 1×3 @ 18″; Cut the back apron.

7. 5 – 1×4 @ 19″; Cut the seat board.

8. 5 – 1×4 @ 15″; Cut the back board.

Step 1:

- *Back legs (see diagram below)*: Mark your chair back legs on the 2 x 4. Be mindful of the back legs at 1½ inches wide in its entirety. One leg will take up the whole 2 x 4.

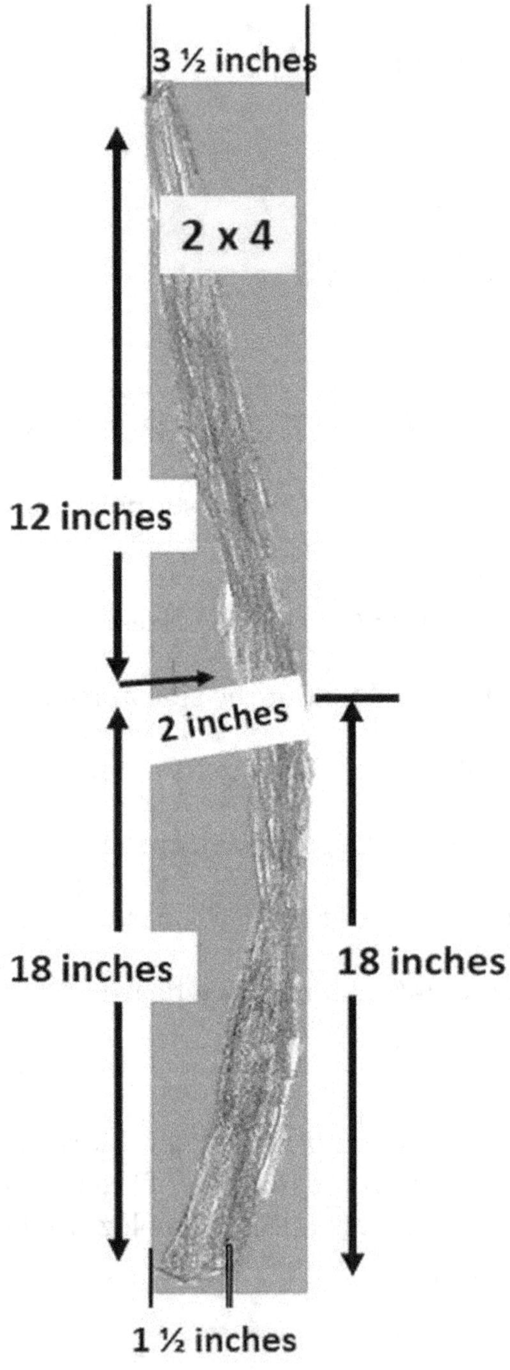
3 ½ inches
2 x 4
12 inches
2 inches
18 inches
18 inches
1 ½ inches

Step 2: Start with building the *back apron* and working your way to the front using a mortise and tenon technique.

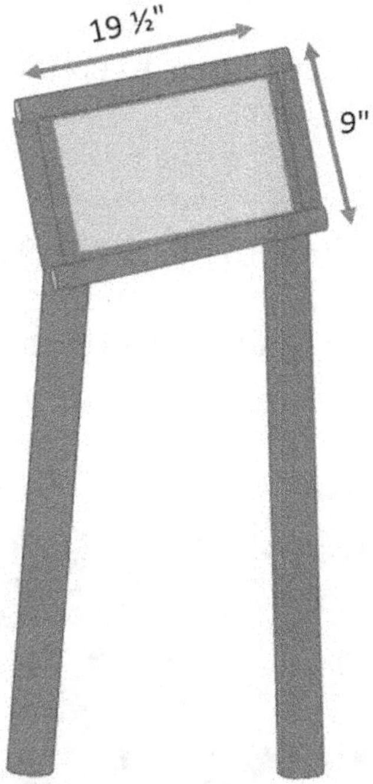

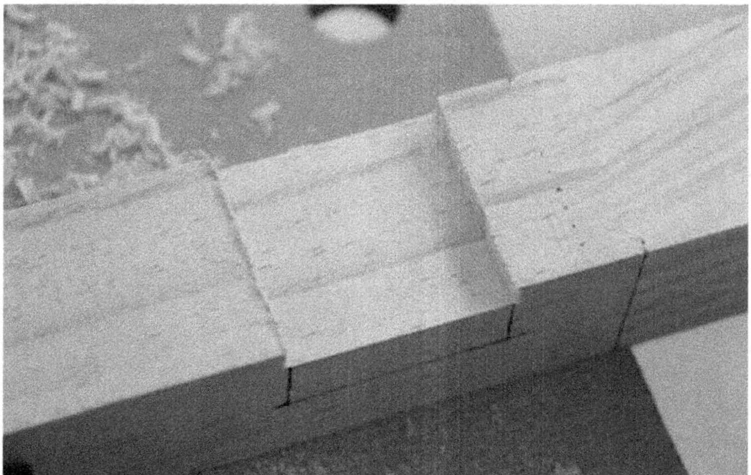

shutterstock.com • 654556528

- 2 – 2×2 @ 19 1/2″; Cut the back supports from these planks.

- Connect the back support by constructing the mortises, and use tenons to connect the back support to the back legs.

Step 3: *Front legs and seat.* Start building the back apron and work your way to the front: *(See figure below)*

- 2 – 2×2 @ 18″; Cut the front legs

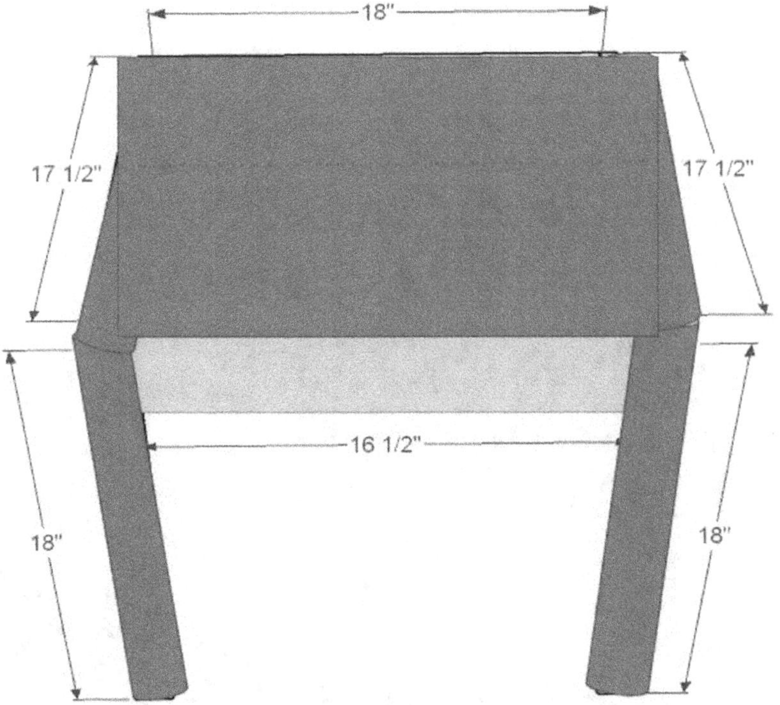

Step 4: Assemble the chair frame. Use a level on the side apron and connect the front of the chair to the back of the chair with mortise and tenons *(see figure below).*

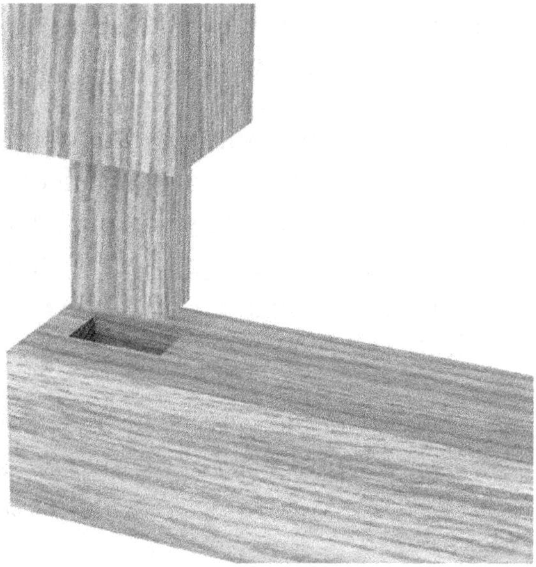

Step 5: Connect your mortise and tenons of the seat boards mindfully to the front and back aprons. Leave a ½-inch gap between each seat board.

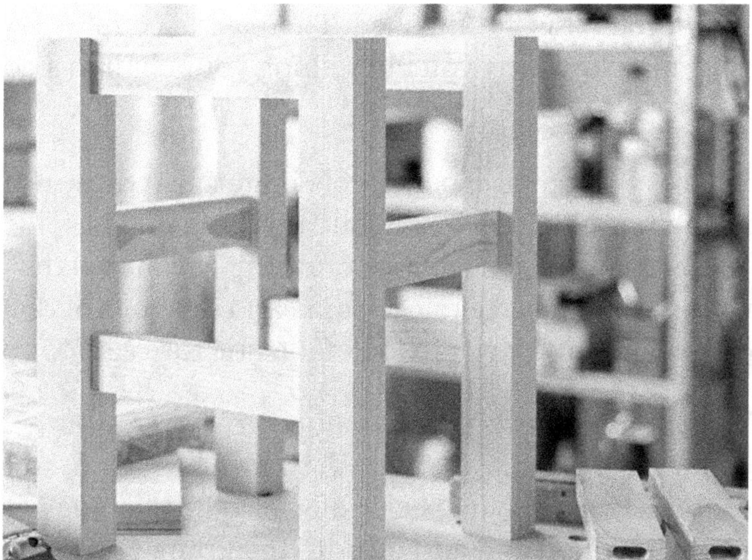

Step 6: Adhere the back boards to the back supports, as you did with the seat boards.

Step 7: Use wood filler for any cracks or holes. Give your new chair a good sanding and finish or stain with your creativity. As a tip, before staining, be sure the chair is free of any dirt or anything sticky. Use a tack cloth in a mix of warm soapy dishwater to clean it off. Rinse with a damp sponge and let it dry all the way.

Step 8: Wipe the surface and legs of your table with mineral spirits, and then apply two coats of stain. Next, apply two coats of semi-gloss polyurethane. Let dry, and you're done!

The Importance of Burnishing

Well you have finished crafting your dining table and chairs, but is it really finished? If you don't want to leave it as raw wood, then it is not finished. There are a couple very important reasons why you burnishing your chair is a good idea.

First of all, wood is a permeable material and very proficient in soaking up just about anything that is spilled on or weathered into it. Finishing your project can seal the timber, keeping oils, chemicals, dirt, and dust out of the wood's grain. You want it to look fantastic for years to come.

The second important reason for burnishing your woodcraft is its grain. Although all timber has grain, some is more vibrant than other species of wood. Burnishing will liven up your wood and add color to the grain. However, it needs a clear-coat application after staining to protect the wood. There are a plethora of finishing types, and some can be used along with others or by itself. There isn't a right or wrong answer here because you will come to find your favorite after experimenting with different looks, desired effects, and application ease.

Paint is a basic finish, but not usually used for covering a beautiful piece of timber. However, there are some semi-transparent paints that, with a very thin coat, will help the grain to exhibit a dramatic effect. It is commonly used on plywood projects. Stain is applied over natural woods to accentuate the grain while still adding some color. Stain can come in dark brown, light brown, red, and other colors. It adds warmth and style to a piece, and it may look quite simple without it.

Clear Coat Finishes

Wax: Easily applied by rubbing and buffing to a shine. It is most effective on fine-grained woods that have already been sanded smoothly. It does not work well on rough-grained timber, such as ash or oak. Wax can also be used as a finish on top of other finishings to repel moisture.

Oils: Also easily applied to finished projects by loading it on and polishing to a dull sheen. The downside of oils is they do not make a shiny finish and can stay sticky for quite a while. However, if this is the way you want to go, you have a few options:

- *Linseed oil:* Can add a richness and warmth in color and increase its moisture resista`nce.
- *Tung oil:* Doesn't shine much, but does protect the wood.

- *Mineral oil:* In food grades, it is good for tending to children's toys and any kitchen appliances.

Shellac: A traditional finish, not commonly used anymore mainly because it doesn't do much in the way of protecting against moisture. It is a resin dissolved in alcohol and brushed onto the surface of the wood. It can be applied to add a natural, amber-looking warmth to your piece.

Varnish: Can be sprayed or smeared on. It does hold up to moisture and is much more durable than other types of stains, such as shellac. Lacquers dry much quicker than any of the oils, this finish dries hard and durable. You don't have to recoat with lacquer, but because it is so hard, it is subject to chipping and cracking with age.

Polyurethane: Gives a strong finish and is a liquid plastic. It comes in matte and glossy finishes and can be applied by brushing, wiping, or spraying. Be sure to use throwaway towels and even disposable brushes, as a solvent has to be used to clean any tools coated with polyurethane. It takes a while to dry, making it vulnerable to collecting dust, so keep this in mind when choosing where to finish your piece.

Polyacrylic: Water-based and dries fast to a durable finish. You can clean your tools with soapy water, so it is easier to use than polyurethane. It is also applied via cloth, brush, or spray.

Chapter Seven: Project 5—Dynamic Bed with Two Dressers

Crafting a dynamic bed and accompanying dressers will allow you to use your Japanese joinery skills and be directly involved in the composition, materials used, and design process. That means no person on the planet will have a bed and set of dressers exactly like yours. A one-of-a-kind bed and dressers set will elevate your interior decor and give you a great sense of pride in its ownership. Controlling the design with your custom joinery has the benefit of you owning a handmade piece that fits your existing furniture. You will not have to compromise on the perfect style, since you can match other pieces you make as well. By making the set yourself, you need only add any adornments or special features you desire. For instance, if there is a joinery element you want to have on your bed, you need only to add them. If you want storage under your bed, you will have it custom-designed by you.

A dynamic bed means a bed with a bold and contemporary design. The shape could be square, octagonal, or pentagonal too. You can continue with the basic rectangle shape too. It is important to understand the complexity before you start, however. Seek the possibilities of making it interesting and not mundane one. The chests can be simple, which will flank the bed. Plan it in reference to the sleeper; it could be for kids, elders, or adults.

Make the design of both the bed and chest. First, finish the bed construction, and then follow it up with two chests to maintain the scale and proportion. Devise an accurate strategy and start the work with minimum effort. Remember to record the time whenever you take up a new project and read the entire plan prior to starting this project. Make sure to craft safely and smartly. Build on a level and clean surface, free of debris or bumps. Check for squares after every section. Use only straight boards and always pre-drill your holes before screwing. For a stronger hold, use finishing nails and glue, making sure to wipe excess glue so it doesn't stain. Most of all, have fun.

Materials:

- 2 x 6 (2; stud length).
- 2 x 4s slats (10; ten feet long).
- Five 2 x 4s (5; stud length for headboard and remaining slat piece).
- 1 x 3 (1; 8 feet long).
- 2-inch screws.
- 2½-inch pocket hole screws (2).
- Wood glue.

Wood Cuts

- Headboard
    - 2 x 6 at 79 inches (6).
    - 2 x 4 at 79 inches (1).
- Back Cleats

- 1 x 3 at 31½ inches (3)

- End
  - 2 x 6 at 61 inches (1).
  - 2 x 4 at 65 inches (1).
- Sides
  - 2 x 4 at 79 inches (2)
  - 2 x 6 at 79 inches (2)
- Slat system
  - 2 x 6 at 79 inches (3).
  - 2 x 4 at 58 inches (11; 4-inch gaps between slats).

Step one: The headboard needs to be attached to the wall so it does not bowl forward. Use a cleat on the back of the headboard *(see diagram below)*.

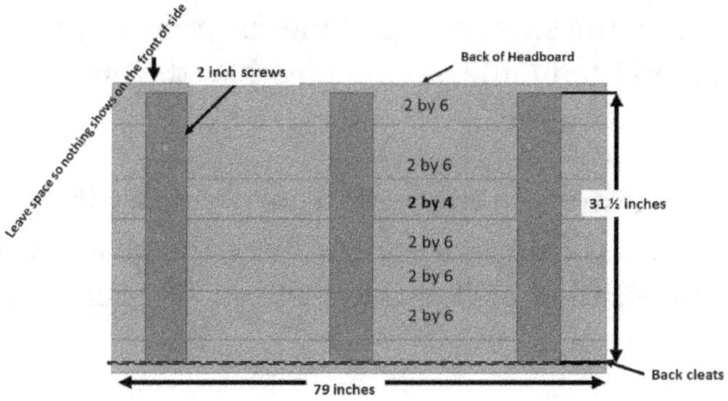

Step 2: Construct two side rails by adhering the 2 x 6 upright pieces to the 2 x 4 platform pieces using one 1½-inch pocket hole and 2½-inch pocket hole screws. Drill pocket holes on the ends at 1½ inches, so you can attach the headboard and footboard later.

Step 3: For the footboard, build the platform top piece so it over extends the upright piece by 2 inches on the ends, keeping everything flush on the back *(see illustration below).*

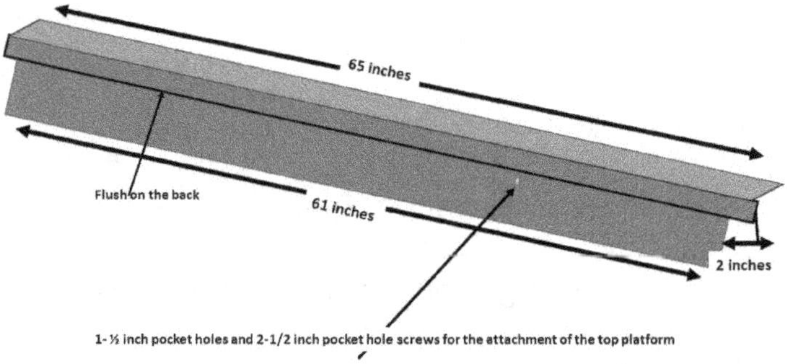

Step 4: Stain the sides and end pieces after they are constructed, and then join the side pieces to the end with 2-½ inch pocket hole screws.

Step 5: Place studs in the wall to keep the headboard in place and prevent it from warping. Adhere the headboard through the pre-drilled pocket holes with 2-½ pocket hole screws.

Step 6: Put the slats in the frame and screw them down.

Step 7: To finish, use wood filler for all holes and leave to dry. Add more if needed. After the filler is completely dry, sand the wood in the direction of the grain using 120 grit sandpaper. Vacuum the bed after sanding and remove any sanding residue. Wipe bed with clean dampened cloth.

Step 8: Apply a sample coat of your chosen finish on a scrap piece to make sure it sticks and and the color is even. Use a wood conditioner or primer if desired. Piece together and ensure color evenness and adhesion. Use a primer or wood conditioner as needed.

Bedroom Chests

Materials:

- ¾-inch plywood 48 x 96 inches (1). Your choice of hardwood: 2 pieces for glide supports, drawers, sides, top, and bottom.
- Hardwood: ¾-inch thick, 12 x 96 inches for the fronts of the drawers (1).
- Hardwood: ¾-inch thick, 3 x 96 inches for the top of the frame (1).
- Hardwood: ¾-inch thick, 2 x 96 inches for the frame face (3).
- Hardwood: ¾-inch thick, 5 x 96 inches for the dividers in the drawers (1).
- Plywood: ¼-inch thick, 48 x 96 inches for the bottom of the drawers and panel on the back (2).
- ¼ lb of 1¼-inch wood screws.
- ⅛ lb of ½-inch wood screws.
- ¼ lb of 1¼-inch Kreg screws.
- Sandpaper.
- Glue.
- Wood filler.
- Polyurethane finish.

Tools

- Power drill with a tapered bit.
- Table saw.
- Band saw.
- Sandpaper at 120 grit and a 320 grit block for finish.
- Tape measure.
- Router with round-over bit.
- Pencil.
- Corner/arc template.
- Miter saw.
- Pocket hole joinery system.
- Screw gun.
- Bar clamps.
- Gripping clamps.

Step 1: Cut the Dresser Box Pieces

A. Using a ¾-inch plywood stock, cut one piece in half, so you have 24 inches. Then, crosscut the 24 x 96 inch in half, and you will have the two sides at 48 inches. With the other half (24 x 96 inches), cut out the bottom panel at 24 x 34½ inches *(see illustration below)*.

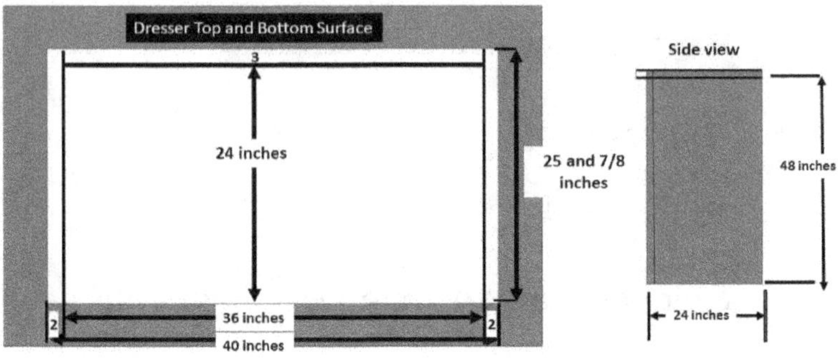

B. *Top panel*: From the plywood stock, cut one piece, 24 x 36 inches.

C. *Pick the top, side, and bottom panels*: On the back edge, make a slot cut (slot cut is also referred to as a daddo cut) a ¼ inch deep by ½ inches to gain the ¼-inch back panel.

D. Pick the 3-inch hardwood stock: Cut one 42 inch piece for the *top frame front panel*; make 45-degree cuts on the ends.

E. Pick the 2 inch hardwood stock and cut two 25⅞ inches for the *top panel sides*; cut one end on each at 45 degrees.

F. Pick the *side panels, top, and bottom* and drill pocket holes down the edges of the panels. Make sure you drill the hole to adhere to the front frame.

G. Pick the ¾ inch plywood stock and cut 8 pieces at 2 ⅞ by 23 ½ for the *slide supports*.

Step 2: Craft the Dresser Box

A. Make the *dresser box* with the four pieces that are used for the *top panel,* found in step one. With glue, pocket hole jig them together. Next, use a band saw and round the front two corners. Then, use a router with a roundover bit to round off the front and side bottom edges (*not* the back edge). Sand them down.

B. Pick the *eight slide supports* and *two side panels.* Use 1¼-inch screws and glue to adhere the supports on the two side panels. Countersink the screws using the dimensions labeled in step one.

C. Pick the *bottom panels, top panels, and two side panels.* Use glue and pocket holes together. Take not of the 2-inch placement of the bottom panel.

Step 3: Craft and Adhere the *Front Frame* Using the 2-Inch *Hardwood* Material

A. Cut two 1½ x 48 inches from the 2-inch material.

B. Cut five 2 x 33 inches from the 2-inch material.

C. Drill pocket holes in the select cut pieces, then sand them down.

D. Using your pocket hole screws and glue, join the pieces.

E. Picking the *front frame* and using your pocket hole screws and glue, join the frame and cabinet.

Step 4: Craft the Drawers Using the Plywood and Hardwood Stock

A. Cut the *front and back panels* from the ¾-inch plywood for the three bigger drawers. Cut six pieces at 9½ x 30½ inches. Next, cut a ¼-inch slot by ⅜ of an inch deep to get the ¼-inch *bottom panel.*

B. Cut the *side panels* from the ¾-inch plywood. For the **three bigger drawers**, cut six pieces at 9½ x 23 ⅞ inches. Next, cut a ¼-inch slot, ⅜ of an inch deep to get the *bottom panel.*

C. Cut the front and back panels from ¾ of an inch plywood for the smaller top drawer. Cut two pieces at 7 x 30½ inches, then cut a ¼-inch slot, ⅜ deep to get the ¼-inch bottom panel.

D. Cut the side panels from the ¾-inch plywood for the smaller top drawer. Cut two pieces at 7 x 23⅞ inches. Cut a ¼-inch slot, ⅜ inches deep to get the ¼-inch bottom panel.

E. Drill two holes in each front and back panel on counter sink holes (center) to get the *drawer center divider.*

F. With the side panels, drill three counter sink holes on each edge.

G. Cut four bottom panels from the ¼-inch plywood stock at 31 x 23⅛ inches. Do so without gluing or fixing. Test the drawers on one panel to make sure your measurements are correct prior to butting the other three bottom panels.

H. Cut four center dividers at 4½ inches by 22⅜ inches from the ¾-inch hardwood stock.

    a. Sand all the pieces.

    b. With glue and 1¼-inch screws, craft all the drawers from all of the pieces.

Step 5: Drawer Slides

A. Attach the slides to the drawers and chest glide support braces.

Step 6: Craft and Adhere the Front of the Drawers

A. Cut three larger drawer fronts from the 12-inch hardwood stock at 11 x 34 inches.

B. Cut one small drawer face at 8½ x 34 inches.

C. Use a router on all edges—even where the finger grabs are—and craft the drawer faces.

D. Center the faces and clamp them on the drawer faces; pre-drill and adhere with 1¼ inch screws.

Step 7: Varnish the Dresser!

A. Cut the back panel from the ¼-inch plywood at 35¼ x 46⅞ inches using the ½-inch screws. Fill any cracks or holes with filler and give all surfaces a final sanding.

B. Put at least three coats of polyurethane on the dresser.

Chapter Eight: Maintenance of Wood and Japanese Lacquering

Japanese lacquer is specific when it comes to maintenance due to the nature of its construction. It is necessary to have a good understanding of how it is made and what elements may contribute to its degradation over time.

Natural lacquer has been produced in Japan for thousands of years and was used as a protective coating for various household times, musical instruments, weapons, and various other cherished items. When it is raw, in Japanese, *urushi* is a milky tree sap, which is then drawn, heated, filtered, and stored. The lacquer's application is a thin layer to a prepared element, such as wood and leather. It is then allowed to preserve in a warm case, free of dust, for more than a day. After polishing, a second layer is applied. Depending on the artist, the piece of work may only have a couple layers or even a hundred layers (Lauern, 2013).

Kijiro Lacquering

Kijiro lacquering is a transparent coating that exposes the grain of the wood for its beauty. As a base, it has a clear to amber coating, with its charm deeply expressed. If you add more coats, the depth will continue to advance, but the grain will be less visible.

Kamakura-Bori Lacquer

Kamakura-Bori lacquer has been a tradition in Japanese joinery dating back to the eleven hundreds. It was used to lacquer altars and Buddhist statues. Finished pieces are called *kamakura-bori*. This type of finish has intentional chisel markings left to liven patterned sections. Another special technique is to scatter black powder on a reddish lacquered surface, so the patterns are noticeable against the darkened background.

Here are the steps to follow:

1. Use knives (of all different shapes) to chisel marking on the surface of your project to accentuate the patterns on the surface.

2. Use the lacquer also as an undercoat. Apply one coat to the whole surface, including any engraved lines or chisel marks.

3. Then, scatter some carbon dust, polishing carbon dust, and polishing talc to maximize the lacquer's effect on the carved surface. This process accentuates the carved, uneven surface.

4. For the middle coat, apply two layers of black urushi lacquer, making sure it does not pool into any of the dents made by your chisel. When it's dry, sand the surface.

5. For the final coat, use a clear Japanese lacquer, and before it is dry, sprinkle makomo powder on the surface.

6. To finish, apply the lacquer again over the entire surface. Let dry and polish to complete the kamakura-bori project!

Fuki-Urushi

Fuki-urushi is a lacquer where the natural glow emphasizes the beauty of the timber's grain.

1. Make sure all fingerprints and dust are removed from the surface of the wood.

2. Apply the lacquer with a brush.

3. Allow the wood to soak up the lacquer, as it will make the grain pattern stand out.

4. Rub it into the wood and let it dry.

5. Carefully polish with sandpaper.

6. Repeat step 2 five times. Note that this process may take a month or more to complete.

Wajima Kirimoto's Sensuji

Wajima Kirimoto's Sensuji technique is created by drenching a cloth with the lacquer and applying it to parts of the wood piece that can be damaged easily. A special brush that creates a bold pattern with many streaks done with jinoko makes for a tough surface and gives the wood an antique feel.

The Honkataji Technique

The *Honkataji* technique is where lacquered clothes are applied to the wood in its natural state and on the areas that are easily damaged, such as the tops of furniture. Then, *jinoko* powder is used as the base coat, it is polished, and a middle coat is added. Once all that is done, a top coat is added. The finished piece will show nine layers of lacquer, leaving the piece always able to be repaired, if damaged.

Caring for Japanese Lacquer

Producing lacquered wood pieces is in depth and takes time and patience. Many special tools and steps are involved in the process. Lacquer can also be colored with minerals or manufactured pigments. For example, iron oxide and cinnabar are combined to make red lacquers. It may also be used in the natural clear state. It can be decorated by adding mother of pearl or metal and polished until the decoration is revealed. Grades of powdered silver and gold with great care are set into the wet lacquer for detail or background effects. However, even though lacquer is hard once manipulated, it can still be damaged. When a lacquered object is in an environment with fluctuating degrees of humidity, lifting and cracking can occur. Therefore, these objects should be handled carefully and with mindfulness when placing them near high moisture areas, cooling and heating vents, or drafty areas. Close attention should be given to how a lacquered object is handled or filled with heavy objects. Too much light can advance a lacquer's degradation, making it lose its durability. Thus, you should make sure you do not expose it to direct sunlight or UV lighting. Watch out for window light by using curtains or filters.

Fingerprints, scratches, and other smudges can damage the lacquer surface. Wear cotton gloves and dust frequently, as some dust particles are abrasive. Never submerge lacquered items in water or use commercial dust removers, such as Endust or Pledge, which can ruin the finish. Lastly, it is imperative to know that Japanese lacquer is not the same at Western shellac. Japanese lacquer is frequently imitated, so be aware; if you are unsure of the lacquer's origin, note that it may be shellac. If it is Japanese lacquer, remember that it is fragile.

To restore the lacquer's appearance, make an overall assessment first, looking for any issues, then use carnauba wax to polish the piece. Apply the wax with one soft cloth, and then polish the item lightly with another clean soft cloth. Do *not* wax pieces that are in good condition. Wood pieces which are lacquered can become insect-infested. A sign of insect infestation includes pin holes surrounded by frass (a sandy-like substance). To remedy this, freezing or fumigating should work.

The best way to care for Japanese lacquerware is to use it periodically because it extends and maintains the integrity of both. Japanese lacquer contains moisture so it shines more after applied. This does not happen with chemical products and therefore, it is a testimony to its authenticity. Be careful handling metals or ceramic products so as to not scratch the fine lacquer.

Dos and Don'ts for Japanese Lacquer

- Don't microwave.
- Don't place it in a dishwasher.
- Don't leave it in the refrigerator for more than an hour or two.
- Do wash by hand with warm, soapy water.
- Don't use abrasive sponges.

- ❖ Don't stack lacquerware.
- ❖ Don't use metal silverware on lacquerware.
- ❖ Do handle with care.

Most individuals can easily feel that a certain piece of furniture has sentimental value, whether it is the dining room set you learned how to craft here or the bedroom set. When you pass these pieces down through the generations, they will bring with them the memories and stories of your past, making them even more valuable to your family. Hardwood furniture made with the Japanese joinery is crafted to be heirloom quality, for it can be revered for future generations. Handcrafted hardwood furniture has a great advantage in its appeal and endurance. The tones and grain patterns of real hardwood bring character and warmth to any room.

At the intermediate level, your skill in finishing will never be matched with veneer. Even when it ages, it becomes part of a very "in-style," rustic look. An old dresser, for instance, can add a stately charm to the master bedroom. As a crafter skilled in Japanese joinery, you can look at a log that has been cut in half and see the graceful diagram of a dining room table beneath the wood's bark. When you see a piece of high-quality wooden furniture with deep dents and other shown damage, you will immediately think of its character, how to bring it back to life, and be eager to start the process. Besides having the ability to become an heirloom, there are many reasons handcrafted furniture is a smarter buy than mass-produced items.

Durability: Furniture built with Japanese joinery is made to tolerate years and years of wear and tear while keeping its natural beauty. It can be finished with protective sealants, making it scratch, stain, and moisture-resistant. Most manufactured furniture is made from plywood or even particle board and quite simply cannot match the longevity of handcrafted hardwood furnishings.

Renewability: Trees of hardwood are renewable resources and add to a healthy environment while they are growing. When harvested, trees drop seed to replace themselves. Unlike mass-produced furniture sets that contain preservatives like formaldehyde or fillers, the hardwood used in crafting the pieces set forth in this book are friendly to the environment. The crafter decides which stains and varnishes they will use and where they are sourced. Pieces can be sourced yourself or from local lumber shops, reducing the cost of transportation and supporting the local economy.

Beauty: Every species of timber has characteristics and grain pattern unique to itself. Even within the same species, wood grain patterns vary from section to section, making every piece of furniture you craft one of a kind. Finishes and stains further add to the luster of the wood.

Customization: Unlike manufactured and mass-produced furniture, hardwood, handcrafted pieces can be created to your own specifications and needs. With options for different stains and finishes and the skill of Japanese joinery techniques, your furniture can be customized to fit your home, style, and preferences.

Restorable. Although hardwood furniture is built to last for generations, the ability to restore it down the road allows it to take on a new life, fit changing style preferences, or match the decor of a new household. Manufactured furniture made of composite material cannot typically be restored and is often discarded when it falls apart or shows significant signs of wear.

Retains its value: Although crafting hardwood furnishing with Japanese joinery techniques can typically be more expensive up front, it certainly holds its value. It retains much more value than manufactured furniture, and down the road, it will end up saving you more money than buying manufactured furniture.

Hopefully by studying this book, you will have increased your skill level and expertise in Japanese joinery. Your knowledge and understanding of Japanese joinery woodworking and how to construct your work has grown exponentially, and hopefully, this book has given you more confidence.

By completing this second book in the series of the Japanese joinery, your skill level has grown, along with the complexity of the pieces you choose to craft. Saving money is not the main impetus for finishing your projects, but it does deserve to be noted because of the expense that you can find with solid wood furniture. Most of all, you will appreciate your work and creativity much more than bringing something home with your debit card. Being involved in designing and creating your own projects with Japanese joinery will lend to it a deeper meaning, as you will know how much work and detail went into every aspect of your creation, leaving you with a great sense of pride and satisfaction. In the future, you will be able to use your Japanese joinery skills to build anything you want that will meet your specific needs.

Anyone who has shopped for furniture has felt the agony of trying to find the right piece to match your vision or accommodate your intentions. Always keep in mind that caring for your tools and keeping them in working order—such as sharpening your knives and wiping them with oil—will be the most important part in your journey with Japanese joinery. Vegetable oil becomes tacky, so you will want to use an oil, such as walnut. Your joinery knowledge should now make you more confident in planning and fitting your furniture into any space perfectly with the exact dimensions necessary, in the exact color, and with any bells and whistles your creative mind desires.

References

Brownell, B. “A History of Wood and Craft in Japanese Design” The Journal of the American

Institute of Architects, 2016. https://www.architectmagazine.com/technology/the-history-of-wood-and-craft-in-japanese-design_o

Butler, L. "Patronage and the Building Arts in Tokugawa Japan", Early Modern Japan. Fall-Winter 2004 https://kb.osu.edu/bitstream/handle/1811/5820/V12N2Butler.pdf;jsessionid=6104A29BFC3D655AA6BCD1605C6DDE80?sequence=1

Hover, B. “How To Find Pearls In Burls”. Wood Magazine.com, 2020. https://www.woodmagazine.com/materials-guide/lumber/wood-figure/how-to-find-earls-in-burls

Hyogo-ken Chijitoroku Ryokogyo. “Japanese Carpentry”. Japanese Guest Houses 2020. https://www.japaneseguesthouses.com/japanese-carpentry/

Kiyosi S. “The Art of Japanese Joinery”. Tankosha, 1978. https://dokumen.pub/the-art-of-japanese-joinery-1nbsped-0834815168-9780834815162.html

Sennet, R. “The Craftsman”, Allen Lane, London, 2008

Toshio Odate. “Japanese Woodworking Tools: Their Tradition, Spirit and Use” (Linden Publishing,Fresno, CA, 2006), p39

Hiroyuki Sugawara. "Oen" 2020. https://the189.com/feature/japanese-woodworker-hiroyuki-sugawara/

Keller, Seth. "Tools we Love: Japanese Ryoba and Mini Dozuki Handsaws". Woodworkers Guild of America, 2020.

www.ingramcontent.com/pod-product-compliance
Lightning Source LLC
LaVergne TN
LVHW010729090726
842905LV00040B/977

* 9 7 8 1 9 5 1 0 3 5 6 8 6 *